THE FLOWERING OF
ABERGLASNEY

THE FLOWERING OF
ABERGLASNEY

GRAHAM RANKIN

ABERGLASNEY ENTERPRISES LTD

PUBLISHED IN 2009 BY ABERGLASNEY ENTERPRISES LTD
ON BEHALF OF ABERGLASNEY RESTORATION TRUST,
LLANGATHEN, CARMARTHENSHIRE SA32 8QH, WALES, UNITED KINGDOM

www.aberglasney.org

ISBN 978 0 9562782 0 3

BRITISH LIBRARY CATALOGUING PUBLICATION DATA
A CATALOGUE RECORD FOR THIS BOOK IS AVAILABLE FROM THE BRITISH LIBRARY

EDITED BY PENNY DAVID
DESIGNED BY MOPUBLICATIONS.COM
PRINTED AND BOUND IN WALES BY GOMER PRESS LTD

Previous pages: *Nomocharis saluenensis*
Opposite: *Maianthemum racemosum* subsp. *amplexicaule*
Following pages: The Tywi in flood near Aberglasney,
with Paxton's Tower and Dryslwyn Castle on the horizon.

ACKNOWLEDGEMENTS

This book has been written not only to celebrate the tenth anniversary of the opening of Aberglasney, but to acknowledge the immense dedication of the trustees, the team of staff and the volunteers who have devoted so much time and skill to making this remarkably ambitious project the success that it has become.

Dedication, skill and generosity have certainly been essential ingredients in what is an extraordinary restoration project. It would not have been possible without the financial help of many organizations and individuals to cover the capital work needed. Particular thanks must be made to Frank and Anne Cabot, whose philanthropy, enthusiasm and commitment have singularly made the restoration of Aberglasney possible.

I would also like to express my particular thanks to Penny David, the editor of this book. Her knowledge and assiduous professionalism have been much needed and enormously appreciated. Finally, I would like to thank the designer Rebecca Ingleby Davies for her skilful creativity.

CONTENTS

FOREWORD

Aberglasney, as an abandoned ruin in the mid 1990s, was irresistible to anyone with the slightest romantic sensibility. Its plethora of walls and walled enclosures had been overwhelmed by Nature. At the same time one sensed a numinous quality – the spirit of those who had created the surroundings in earlier centuries and who had cared deeply about their creation.

Restoration would mean removing all the adventitious greenery that clothed the structures. The result would be a denuded labyrinth and it would be years before the romantic green mantle returned – this time, it was hoped, as the best possible ensemble of horticultural treasures.

A garden is as good as the persons who devote their lives to its creation and nurture. How then to find the best possible horticultural leadership for Aberglasney? I elected to write to those horticultural luminaries in the UK whom I had met over the years and ask for their suggestions. Among many cordial replies was a note from Tony Schilling, the former Director of Wakehurst Place and Deputy Director of Kew, suggesting that we approach Graham Rankin – in his view one of the best and hardest working horticulturists in the UK. In short order Graham, and his talented horticulturist wife Frances, were on board.

In retrospect it was the perfect solution for Aberglasney. Graham and Frances have won the hearts of Carmarthenshire and the ever-growing circle of friends of Aberglasney abound, not only in Britain, but around the world.

Graham Rankin is a rare bird. He combines consummate horticultural savvy and plantsmanship with masterful administrative skills, as well as a keen aesthetic sensibility. This book is evidence that he is an accomplished photographer as well.

Graham and Frances have devoted some ten years of their lives to Aberglasney and many changes have been wrought. The changes have been dramatic and are chronicled in this book. However, as Aberglasney devotees well know, this is only the beginning, a first report on the horticultural excitement that proceeds apace. There will be updates periodically and, in due course, Aberglasney will recover its romantic mantle and, given its extraordinary setting and horticultural brilliance, will take its place in the top ranks among the outstanding gardens of the world. Fortunately, its numinosity is very much intact, if not greater than ever!

Frank Cabot

A view of the mansion's west façade taken by Frank Cabot on his 1994 visit.

PREFACE

Soon after it was confirmed that I was taking on the position at Aberglasney at the beginning of 1999, I started delivering vanloads of 'treasured' plants that I had acquired or propagated over many years. If anyone had any doubts about my enthusiasm, the constant accumulation of plants being deposited outside the office was a testament to my obsession.

It was a premature exercise, as restoration was still going on apace. The gathered multitude of botanical specimens had to be kept for a minimum of nine months in pots or 'heeled in' before any of them could be planted in a prepared area of garden. They were an eclectic mixture; some were remarkably rare, collected many years previously, others were of purely sentimental value. Nevertheless, they were all far too precious to me to leave behind and Aberglasney seemed the right resting place for them.

Thankfully I am not alone in my passion for plants; a growing number of people share the same interest in plants and gardens, some to the point of being obsessive. The National Council for the Conservation of Plants and Gardens bears witness to this. There are now a remarkable 660 national plant collections in Britain and Ireland, half of which are in private ownership and cover genera from *Abelia* to *Zingiber*.

Unlike some historic gardens, Aberglasney is not stuck in a time warp. With the exception of the Cloister Garden, the new planting does not reflect the garden's antiquity, but looks to the future. The development of the garden will continue to showcase the very best varieties that plant breeders create and will also cultivate some of the most recent plant introductions as plant collectors discover new and exciting species in the wild.

Among the most enjoyable elements of my work are my plant-hunting expeditions. These consist of occasional journeys around the country visiting specialist nurseries to procure new and exciting specimens for the garden. The trips are well planned in advance, having worked out a route using that indispensable publication, the RHS *Plant Finder*. The golden era of plant-hunting may have passed, but every year valuable new plant species are being introduced along with numerous excellent new cultivars. I feel that the general public are conned by some plant retailers who continually churn out the

same inferior plants year after year, when there are so many better forms available.

Many visitors to Aberglasney comment on the garden's unique atmosphere, which is very nice to hear, but what gives me the greatest pleasure is seeing visitors experiencing the same delight in the treasures grown in the garden that I do, not just the visual aspect, but the fragrance of flowers and leaves, the touch of velvet-covered buds and seed heads and the excitement of seeing something new for the first time.

A recent experiment revealed that average walking speeds in cities around the world have increased by around ten per cent in the last few years. I hope that the words and more importantly the images in this book will inspire garden visitors to look with renewed interest at what is around them, to awaken their senses and to slow down. A passing glance does not do justice; it takes time to fully appreciate the magnificence and beauty that plants and gardens have to offer.

Graham Rankin

13

CHAPTER ONE

A GARDEN LOST IN TIME

Aberglasney stands just over 60 metres above sea level, nestled in the saddle between two hills on a ridge overlooking the Tywi valley to the south. Grongaer Hill, the higher of the two and an Iron Age hill fort, lies to the west. The Tywi valley is an area of great historical interest, its margins punctuated with remains of ancient castles. Dinefwr Castle is two miles to the east of Aberglasney and Dryslwyn is two miles to the west, on the boundary of the parish of Llangathen. Dinefwr has existed since the late twelfth century and was once the capital seat of the kingship of Deheubarth (*deheu* means 'of the south'). One of the kingdom's royal sons, Owain Glyndŵr, proclaimed himself Prince of Wales and led a rebellion against Wales's overlords until his death in 1416.

But where to begin Aberglasney's complicated story? For me it began in 1999, when I was lured to the lovely Tywi valley in Carmarthenshire by the temptation of an improbable new garden restoration project which was in search of someone to re-create a garden in a historic and romantic setting. I knew Wales well, and would have travelled along the A40, unknowingly passing Aberglasney en route to Pembrokeshire on many occasions. The beauty of Carmarthenshire was a part of Wales yet to be discovered. It transpired that Aberglasney was new to practically everyone. A forgotten historic garden feature had been rediscovered near the old mansion, a structure so important that it had inspired an unprecedented restoration campaign, as well as a colossal amount of research, discussion and argument.

The root cause of all this was a courtyard surrounded by rows of arches creating a raised walkway – all but unrecognizable in its state of decay. This architectural conundrum

was the source of much debate. Garden historians had many conflicting views as to its origin and purpose and years of deliberation ensued. Eventually, after extensive restoration, the structures' true architectural form was made clearly visible. The Cloister Range and Parapet Walk are now considered to be a rustic version of a rare Renaissance survival, unique in the British Isles and with very few examples remaining in other parts of Europe.

The style of the raised walkway was once very popular throughout Europe and typified an Italianate garden style which was at its most fashionable during the early seventeenth century. Examples are known to have existed at Moor Park and Massey's Court, both of which were later swept away by a 'Capability Brown' makeover.

Maybe it was sheer disbelief that was to blame for the long-drawn-out scepticism voiced by garden historians. How could such an important structure be unearthed in a

Previous pages: The unique Cloister Garden prompted Aberglasney's whole restoration process. Here early-flowering *Tulipa schrenkii* bejewels the re-created grass parterre

Above: The crumbling west façade of the mansion in 1994 shrouded in vegetation, including a semi-mature western red cedar growing from a first-floor window.

Opposite: The Tywi near Aberglasney, looking upstream towards the Brecon Beacons, with Dinefwr Castle on the horizon.

remote part of southwest Wales? What makes this find even more remarkable is the fact that only just a few miles down the road at Newton House, one of the most quintessential of landscapes in the style of Capability Brown was executed in Dinefwr Park.

The rolling pastoral landscape certainly took people by storm during the eighteenth century. It is a peculiar irony that one member of the Dyer family who lived at Aberglasney in the early eighteenth century is renowned for his writing on the picturesque landscape, in which such formality would have been frowned upon. If finances had been plentiful at the time, the cloister range could well have been razed to the ground to keep up with fashion, but instead, hundreds of tonnes of spoil were deposited in the cloistered area to soften its formality.

By the 1990s, all that was left were the gravity-defying remnants of stone walls, bound together by dense vegetation that smothered their entirety. An upper storey of self-sown ash and sycamore trees populated the grounds and specimens grew out of every conceivable crevice in the masonry. It is understandable why it was considered by most, quite literally beyond restoration.

The unimaginable concept of saving and possibly restoring the crumbling structures at Aberglasney was initiated and driven by one man, William Wilkins, the visionary not only behind Aberglasney, but also behind the National Botanic Garden of Wales at Middleton Hall, a historic site eight miles west of Aberglasney at Llanarthne.

The artist William Wilkins is a man of remarkable talent and foresight with a tenacious determination. The Peter Marshall quotation 'Let us not be content to wait and see what will happen, but give us the determination to make the right things happen' could well be his motto. His passion

about the rescue and restoration of Aberglasney was quite extraordinary – and extraordinarily persuasive.

In 1993 William Wilkins gave a talk on Welsh gardens to the New York-based Garden Conservancy. In the small audience were Frank Cabot – founder of the Garden Conservancy, and himself a brilliant garden-maker – and his wife Anne. As hosts for the evening, they took the speaker out to dinner, and took the opportunity of quizzing him. Two of the Welsh gardens discussed had made a strong impression on Frank Cabot. One was Plas Brondanw, Clough Williams-Ellis's legendary garden in north Wales, and the other was a romantic ruin called Aberglasney.

William Wilkins had implied in his talk that a stalemate in Aberglasney's fortunes offered a rare chance to save the site. Aberglasney was a listed building, yet the columns of its Victorian portico had been put up for auction at Christie's. By law they had to be reinstated; a huge expense for the current owners. Encumbered by this legal millstone, the property might be bought for a favourable amount – and then, it was hoped that a trust could be formed to undertake its restoration.

Right, above: The façade of the mansion at its nadir in the 1990s, showing the scar where the Victorian portico had been removed.

Right: Excavation of the extensive cobbling between the Gatehouse and the Cloister Garden in 1999, with William Wilkins keenly watching progress.

Opposite: The luxuriant Tywi valley seen from Dryslwyn Castle, with Dinefwr on its hilltop in the centre.

Frank and Anne Cabot expressed an interest, and – in practical vein – suggested asking the landscape architect Hal Moggridge to take a look at Aberglasney: they had previously worked together on what Frank Cabot calls 'a failed effort to salvage the gardens at Fulham Palace in Hammersmith'. Hal Moggridge, who was already collaborating with William Wilkins on Middleton, came up with an enthusiastic report on the quality of the ruins at Aberglasney and the potential to re-create an interesting garden. Frank and Anne Cabot followed with a visit to Aberglasney in January 1994. Witnessing for themselves the imminent disappearance of over 400 years of history and the entrancing atmosphere of the place, they undertook to fund the acquisition of the property.

The foresight and dogged enthusiasm of William Wilkins and the conviction, vision and remarkable philanthropy of Frank and Anne Cabot were magical ingredients. Their legacy is what can be seen today.

Above: Aberglasney nestled in the saddle between two hills, with the church of St Cathen on the right of the picture.

Right: Growing at the entrance to the garden, the handsome *Magnolia obovata* greets visitors in June and July with a strong, fruity fragrance from its parchment-coloured flowers.

A NEW BEGINNING

Aberglasney Restoration Trust was set up in May 1994. Experts of every kind were summoned, and funding was obtained from various sources. A vast project of clearance, evaluation and rebuilding began three years later. Early on a team from BBC Wales began recording the process on film. The series of programmes broadcast in 1999 just as the garden was being opened to the public was entitled *Aberglasney: A Garden Lost in Time*. The name echoed the 'Lost Gardens of Heligan', the Cornish project that virtually launched the trend for rediscovering and reviving forgotten gardens a few years earlier. It would perhaps be more accurate to say the garden at Aberglasney was *found* just in time for restoration to save it. People were fascinated by the unfolding of the story, and the publicity generated put Aberglasney on the map and attracted good numbers of visitors.

Aberglasney is both old and new. The brown tourist road signs have been up only ten years, but over six centuries ago a poet was writing about 'nine green gardens' hereabouts. It would more or less be possible to count nine gardens here today (depending on what you chose to define as a separate garden), but they are unlikely to coincide with those medieval poetic enclosures.

Left: During a cold spell in winter the water tumbling down the retaining wall behind the mansion has this *Dryopteris erythrosora* frozen in time.

Right: Aberglasney offers many opportunities to experiment with new introductions. The divinely elegant *Schefflera taiwaniana*, discovered by Bleddyn and Sue Wynn-Jones in 1996, thrives at the foot of the slope behind the mansion, where it has survived low temperatures with no sign of stress.

Above: The calm north façade Aberglasney presents to the world today, its Victorian portico restored and the trimmed Yew Tunnel at far right.

Right: View of the rear of the mansion in 2004, showing the ruinous east wing. Grongaer Hill – made famous by John Dyer's poems – fills the skyline to the west.

Another poet in the eighteenth century praised Aberglasney's terrace walks, lakes and other features, but we can't be sure exactly what he saw. Whatever the earlier owners built, the last great phase of remodelling came in the 1840s, when the house was embellished with the colonnaded portico and the old Queen Anne façade adjusted to accommodate it.

The architecture is not outstanding, and the addition of the portico is of questionable merit. However, that portico played an important role in the reversal of Aberglasney's apparently doomed fortunes as restoration became a possibility in the mid 1990s. It has become part of Aberglasney's identity, and tells part of Aberglasney's story as surely as do the other historic features you see as you approach the house, the famous Yew Tunnel, and the Gatehouse Tower.

ABERGLASNEY'S FAMILIES

How much do you need to know about a garden when you visit? You can enjoy the setting and, of course, the plants (now that there *are* plants at Aberglasney). But Aberglasney is a special case, and it helps considerably to know some background – to know how it came to be as it is.

The history of Aberglasney and its families is the subject of *A Garden Lost in Time*, subtitled *The Mystery of the Ancient Gardens of Aberglasney*, first published in 1999. (The softback edition of 2000 is updated with an additional chapter.) Its author, Penny David, tells 'the story so far' in great detail and readers are referred to that informative book for a fuller account of Aberglasney's intriguing back-story. Here I've chosen to highlight just a few stepping stones – sufficient to illuminate a path through the garden's history.

It is thought that one of the early owners of a dwelling where Aberglasney now stands was Rhydderch ap Rhys, the great-grandson of Llywelyn Foethus, Lord of Llangathen. Lewis Glyn Cothi, one of the greatest of the fifteenth-century Welsh bards, wrote an ode to Rhydderch describing his home:

He has a proud hall, a fortress made
 bright with whitewash,
and encompassing it all around
 nine green gardens.
Orchard trees and crooked vines,
 young oaks reaching up to the sky.

It is now generally accepted that this earlier dwelling stood more or less where the present mansion stands today. Some of the existing building certainly contains medieval

THE YEW TUNNEL

Victorians used to visit Aberglasney to admire the venerable Yew Tunnel on the North Lawn. Unpruned since the 1950s, wayward branches grew taller than the mansion and in windy conditions threatened to break the tunnel's back. In November 2000 – despite protests from tree-huggers – we began a phased programme of drastic pruning, trimming the top from a 'cherry-picker' (below), which gave great views over the Cloister Garden (above right). But yew responds well, and the tunnel has now healthily regained its compact outline (below right): the specimen tree in the foreground is *Tilia henryana*. The final phase of work in 2005 revealed the full glory of the fused trunks on the western side (centre), the result of young yews being originally planted as a hedge against a wall.

Above: In the absence of historic documents, artistic licence conjures Bishop Rudd's Cloister Garden as it might have been. Architect Craig Hamilton drew this pastiche in the style of the period, including two-storey towers at either side which have not been reinstated.

Opposite: The man behind Aberglasney's ambitious layout: Anthony Rudd, Bishop of St David's from 1594 to 1614, who began building here around 1600. His effigy lies in a fine bedstead tomb in Llangathen parish church.

elements, and medieval culverts run underneath the Cloister Garden. But all of this is now hidden, although its archaeology has been recorded.

For the story of the existing gardens, the first notable occupant of Aberglasney was a Yorkshireman, Anthony Rudd. A high-flying cleric, he became Dean of Gloucester in 1584 and was appointed Bishop of St David's in 1594. Apart from his role at Aberglasney, he is remembered for two reasons: he had a brush with the ageing Queen Elizabeth over a

sermon, and survived the encounter; and after his death in 1614 he was commemorated in a magnificent bedstead tomb which can still be seen in Llangathen parish church. The bishop bought Aberglasney around 1600 (frustratingly, we have not been able to discover exactly when) and soon acquired several other properties in Carmarthenshire. Acquiring land (and marrying well) was (then, as now) the thing to do. Bishop Rudd hoped to establish a dynasty here, and his son Sir Rice Rudd shared this ambition until the Civil War devastated his fortunes. According to an early account, Bishop Rudd built 'a handsome seat' at Aberglasney. No contemporary mentioned his Cloister Garden, but archaeology has pinpointed its construction to the first decades of the seventeenth century.

The next notable family to occupy Aberglasney were the Dyers, who purchased the estate from the impoverished Rudds around 1710, and produced Aberglasney's one real celebrity, the poet John Dyer. His father, Robert Dyer, was a wealthy solicitor in nearby Carmarthen, and is reported to have 'rebuilt' Aberglasney. It is not known quite how extensively he renovated the Rudds' house, but there is no doubt that before he died in 1720 he was responsible for imposing a smart new north façade in Queen Anne style.

John Dyer was born in the nearby village of Llanfynydd in 1699 and during his early years lived at Aberglasney, of which he was evidently very fond: in his poem *The Country Walk* he called it 'The poet's pride, the poet's home'. He was educated at Westminster, and then worked in his father's practice. He gave up the law on his father's death to take up art, studying in London and in Italy. He travelled as an itinerant artist, and in 1726 published the poem *Grongar Hill*, which earned him a reputation not only as a

Above: The rear of the mansion housing the service quarters was completely derelict when the Aberglasney Restoration Trust took over.

Opposite, above: Mud, glorious mud? The view east over the Pool Garden on my first day was enough to damp anyone's spirits. Beyond the pool, the hessian-draped Parapet Walk, and the scaffolded mansion.

Opposite, below: Every stage of the restoration was recorded by BBC camera crews for the TV series *A Garden Lost in Time*. Despite mud, scaffolding and machinery, the rebuilding of the Ionic portico on the north façade of the mansion in early 1999 proved to be one their liveliest sequences.

poet, but also as the 'godfather' of the picturesque movement ('picturesque' comes from the Italian *pittoresco*, 'in the manner of a painting'). In the event John Dyer's lasting fame rests on the word-pictures he painted in his poetry rather than on his paintings, and the scenery around Aberglasney, particularly Grongaer Hill, is forever associated with his vision.

Even Dyer's poetry has come to seem archaic. William Wordsworth said of his longest poem, *The Fleece*, that 'in parts it was superior to any writer in verse since John Milton, for imagination and purity of style', but it makes hard reading nowadays. Two recently published editions of Dyer's works edited by John Goodridge – *Selected Poetry and Prose* (2000) and *The Fleece* (2007) – provide introductions and explanatory notes that help to put Dyer in context for the modern reader. John Dyer is an engaging and complex character, brought to life by Belinda Humfrey's profile in the 'Writers of Wales' series (1980). However, he passed the greater part of his life elsewhere, and we must concentrate on Aberglasney.

In 1798 the last of the Dyer family put the property on the market for £10,000 guineas. It was eventually sold in 1803 to Thomas Phillips, a local man who had made a fortune as a surgeon in the East India Company, and it remained in his family for 150 years. Some repairs and refurbishments were carried out to the property in the early 1800s, but we know of no significant change to the gardens. When Thomas Phillips's nephew John Walters inherited in 1824, he did make a number of 'improvements'. He probably added the portico to the façade of the mansion – it played a key role in Aberglasney's recent fate – when he became High Sheriff of Carmarthenshire in 1841. He also added to his name, and became John

Walters Philipps. For the rest of the century and Victoria's reign, Aberglasney experienced a new heyday. The walled gardens and a state-of-the art range of glasshouses, each designed for a different purpose, would have been fine-tuned by an expert head gardener and his team to grow the greater part of the household's food crops. The Parapet Walk around the Cloister Garden would have become fashionable again in the Victorian climate of revivalism. An article featuring the Yew Tunnel in the *Gardeners Chronicle* magazine of 1898 described it in passing as Jacobean.

But two World Wars changed the old order, and by the middle of the twentieth century most estates like this were simply no longer viable. Many old country houses became institutions such as schools or convalescent homes, and a number were pulled down, while their surrounding land was divided up and sold off. In 1977 the Aberglasney estate was eventually split up and auctioned in several lots.

An entrepreneurial couple, with the intention of restoring some of the building, purchased the mansion, but the daunting task became too burdensome. It was the sale at Christie's of the already partially collapsed portico from the north façade of the Grade II* mansion, that brought the desperate plight of Aberglasney to the attention of the public. A court case ensued, and eventually the portico was returned and an enforcement notice was served on the owners to undertake repairs. Defeated and dejected, they eventually sold the property in 1995 to the Aberglasney Restoration Trust for the sum of £35,000. Since that time, five further acquisitions have been made to piece back most of the core of Aberglasney's ancillary buildings, including most of the buildings of the adjacent Home Farm.

A BAPTISM OF FIRE, AND MUD

The initial phase of structural restoration was intended to be nearing completion when I arrived on the scene in the spring of 1999. I found myself plunged into a different world. I had been happily working away in charge of the garden restoration of a private estate in Surrey when I was told about this new project in Wales where they wanted someone to create a rather special new garden virtually from scratch. The garden was committed to opening in July. Restoration of the house and structural elements of the garden had been under way for the past two years or so, and was by no means complete. It was not a case of creating a garden, but getting the grounds suitable for people to walk around in safety and a degree of comfort.

Having worked for the previous fourteen years alongside grooms, caretakers, chauffeurs and domestics, I now found myself working alongside huge teams of building contractors, supervisors, garden contractors, archaeologists and an army of consultants. The financial implications of engaging all these specialists was both staggering and bewildering. I was taken aback when I discovered that a consultant's hourly rate equated to half the weekly wage of a trained gardener, not to mention the added-on costs of first-class rail travel, overnight accommodation and numerous other disbursements.

The situation got worse before it got better. Two principal companies involved with the work ceased to exist before their contracts were completed, leaving tasks unfinished and the financial predicament of needing to rectify their defective work. Fortunately the outside world was totally oblivious to this situation and apart from developments being a little slower than usual,

Above: The Parapet Walk, with its continuation as the retaining wall above the Upper Walled Garden, provides an excellent vantage point for visitors. The sparse foreground planting has grown beyond recognition since Aberglasney held its official opening in July 1999.

Opposite: HRH the Prince of Wales first visited Aberglasney in July 2001, when restoration of the Cloister Garden was still under way. Here he discusses the restoration of the pitched stone pathways.

it just appeared as if work was 'in progress'.

One of the aspects that distressed me most – apart from the cost of inefficient contractors – was the consequence for the garden. To a gardener soil is a precious commodity, the basis of everything that grows. Many areas of the garden at Aberglasney had been worked for centuries by careful backbreaking hand cultivation, which in time would have produced a soil that was both intensely fertile and friable.

Sadly this had been destroyed by careless use of heavy earthmoving machinery by contractors in sodden conditions during the early stages of ground clearance, to me an unforgivable misdemeanour. Perhaps it's easy to criticize in retrospect – they had a huge job on their hands and more importantly a looming deadline for completion – but a little more forethought and planning would have prevented much of the damage and later work on rectifying the problems of soil quality.

ENTER THE VISITORS

The date of the official opening of Aberglasney was set as the third of July 1999, and we opened to the public a day later. A long list of dignitaries was invited, including numerous sponsors and distinguished guests. Verse was read by the Welsh actor Daniel Evans, songs sung by Shân Cothi and Gillian Clarke recited her own specially commissioned poetry. It was a most memorable day, and these events, too, became part of the television series. This was tremendous publicity, and from the opening in July to the end of the season in October, 32,000 people visited Aberglasney.

It is, however, a little ironic that on the date of the opening, there was hardly a garden to be seen. Apart from new planting in the two walled gardens, endless walls, a basic path network and acres of brown earth was all that was evident. I recall some unsuspecting early visitors being somewhat disillusioned, having paid the entrance fee to a garden, to actually see nothing more than a building site and naked walls.

However, the majority of visitors who made a visit in the early days were fascinated with what they saw – a rare opportunity not only to see a garden being created from a blank canvas, but a house being brought back to life and archaeologists still at work unearthing new discoveries to reveal Aberglasney's long history on a daily basis. Most gardens you visit have been around a hundred years or so at least. To see a garden actually being created in front of your eyes is quite something. People responded positively to seeing 'work in progress', and were very often inspired to make repeat visits to inspect developments. Many of the original visitors are still coming, because there is always something new to see.

By the autumn, most of the remaining

contracted workforce had completed their tasks and moved on, allowing the long awaited peace and tranquillity to return to the garden. There was a welcome break during the winter, which gave the gardeners an opportunity to undertake further landscaping work, unimpeded by the visiting public.

The garden opened again the following April, but as we approached autumn, it seemed a pity to close for nearly half the year. I don't consider any garden complete unless it is planted for year-round interest. And then it becomes logical to invite visitors in to share your pleasure with others. Although the

newly cultivated areas were far from mature, the historic structures still looked very impressive. Curious members of the public continued to want to see what was going on. I decided to open the garden on the first Sunday of each month during the winter. Traditionally most gardens that open to the public close during the winter months, depriving visitors of the chance of appreciating what can be seen. Not only are flowers of interest, but this is by far the best time to appreciate the variations of bark and evergreen leaves, the form of coniferous trees, persistent fruits which glow in the

Above: The wooded areas at Aberglasney provide a perfect habitat for choice exotic plants that enjoy the same conditions. Here a grafted specimen of *Rhododendron* 'Fortune' is being planted in Pigeon House Wood in the early spring of 1999.

Above right: Beside a path leading up to the Alpinum, a planting of wintersweet (*Chimonanthus praecox* var. *luteus*) scents the air. Its carpet of snowdrops survives from the days before restoration began.

Opposite: Snow brings a dramatic beauty to the tree ferns and bridge, innovations introduced into Bishop Rudd's Walk in 1999.

winter sunshine and glistening frosted seed heads. Winter is also the best time to see the structure and architecture of the garden.

We continued opening the garden at regular intervals during the winter months. However, with the opening of the Shop and plant centre complex in June 2003, it became possible to admit visitors on a regular basis. Since 2003 the garden and the café have remained open throughout the year, with the exception of Christmas Day and periods of exceptionally severe weather.

On New Year's Day there are usually more than thirty different plants in flower in the

garden, and by the end of February that number has at least doubled. One of the nicest winter combinations can be found as you head uphill from the southern doorway in the Upper Walled Garden, passing the seductively fragrant *Chimonanthus praecox*, the wintersweet, on your left. In his book *Adventures of a Gardener*, Sir Peter Smithers describes wintersweet as 'having a first-class sexy scent if ever there was one.' I will let you decide for yourself. Here, beneath our wintersweet, the ground is carpeted with snowdrops, one of the few plants that survived the years of neglect.

CHAPTER TWO

THE CLOISTER GARDEN

One of the comments I hear from visitors in the Cloister Garden is: 'It's in remarkably good condition for its age.' If only they had seen it in the not-too-distant past. I can easily excuse them for making such a mistake, and always take it as a compliment to how well the restoration was done.

This historic garden is, of course, quite unique, and merits a brief description here. The western range – the base of the 'U'-shaped plan and the Cloister Range proper – provides a dignified, lofty, covered walking space some fifty paces long. The technical name for this feature is 'cryptoporticus', which means an enclosed gallery. Someone has drawn a parallel with the 'long gallery' characteristic of many Tudor houses, where exercise could be taken in inclement weather. The two flanking ranges lack this ground-level walkway, but are pierced with curious low arches. The whole massive structure supports a majestic raised walkway around three sides of the enclosure; the house closes the fourth side.

Today it does seem incredible that such a massive feat of architectural stonework can have been overlooked by history. 'What did they mean, a garden "lost" in time?' visitors ask. 'How could you "lose" something like this?'

Previous pages: It is hard to imagine that little over a decade ago the elegant Cloister Garden was so derelict as to be unrecognizable. The areas of paving correspond to those discovered by archaeologists, but the grass and gravel parterre is a copy of a typical period design

Opposite: The fragrant *Tulipa sylvestris* growing in the grass of the parterre.

Right: View towards the southwest corner of the Cloisters.

Left: When weeds masked the cloister arches in the western range and blurred the crumbling walkway, it was hard to appreciate the sheer scale of the structures.

Opposite page: The Cloister Garden after archaeological investigation, revealing the remaining area of diaper-patterned pathway in the exposed archway (far right). The indentations of the same pattern are visible continuing right across the garden. The elongated trenches are thought to have been created by extensive cultivation before the 1600s. The long channel was formed in the nineteenth century, when a small fountain was built in the centre of the garden.

Two coins found during excavation in the Cloister Garden: a long-cross silver penny dating to Edward I (1282–1289) and a silver half-groat dating back to Henry VII.

Even I sometimes have to pinch myself to be reminded what happened. You have to look at photographs of the 'before' stage, and of the restoration process, to understand the transformation. The cloister structures were in bad repair – the parapets had collapsed, and seedling trees were bursting from the stonework; in the courtyard the ground level had been raised over the years, and this higher level was being augmented by tonnes of fallen masonry. Finally, the whole was blanketed with at least forty years' worth of rampant vegetation.

The first stage was to clear the jungle. One might be forgiven for assuming that the Cloister Garden housed the National Collection of Japanese knotweed, as well as flourishing crops of brambles, ivy, seedling trees and weeds of every kind. During the archaeological excavation, well over 100 tonnes of spoil had to be removed. Because

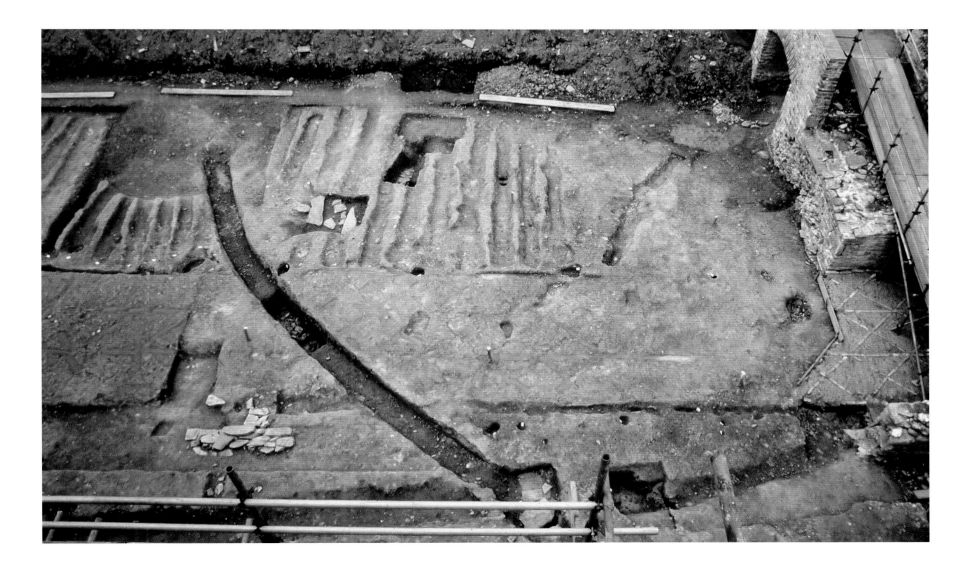

this contained knotweed roots, it was classified as contaminated waste, making its disposal both time-consuming and exorbitantly expensive. It took several seasons to eradicate what remained, using a systemic herbicide and persistent removal of the roots by careful excavation. No one knows how the knotweed arrived in the Cloister Garden. When it was first introduced to Britain in 1825, it was considered a valuable ornamental, but it is too tall to have been intentionally planted in such a confined area. I suspect that it was inadvertently brought in from elsewhere at some point when the ground levels here were raised during a nineteenth-century makeover.

Once this extraneous material had been removed, the real archaeology could begin. As the *raison d'être* of the entire restoration project, the cloister ranges caused more

intrigue and puzzlement than any other part of the garden. Archaeologists and historians have debated their age, origins and intended use, often with very differing opinions.

Within the Cloister Garden there is evidence of medieval masonry, including a stone-arched culvert, which carries the water from the spring originating from the cellar under the mansion. It is also thought that the outer walls of the cloister range were once defensive walls and were built long before the cloisters were added to them. The sloping batter at the base of the northern and western walls certainly suggests an earlier period, along with silver coinage found in the Cloister Garden, which dated back to the thirteenth century.

The cloister range is now generally accepted to be an authentic example of a typical garden structure dating back to the early seventeenth century and is considered to be the only one that remains in the UK. It is assumed that the west wing of the Cloister Garden was built around 1600 by Bishop Anthony Rudd, and that the two wings were built or completed by his son, Sir Rice Rudd, who inherited the property some fifteen years later and lived here until the 1660s. It is for this reason that in completing the restoration,

Above: The recently restored cloister walls in 1999, draped in hessian and blue sheeting to protect them from inclement weather.

Below: During the restoration, the team of archaeologists left no stone unrecorded, their findings often filling gaps in the documentary evidence. Here the diaper-patterned path from the Gatehouse to the Cloister Garden is being mapped: the paving on either side has since been preserved under grass.

we consulted garden fashions up to 1620 and looked at plants available in that period.

Despite an extensive and thorough archaeological investigation during 1998–1999, no original detail of the early seventeenth-century garden design could be found. Some clues to the extent of the path surfaces were indicated by areas of random pitched stone. But one of the most exciting areas to be uncovered in 1998 was a two-metre length of ornate diaper-patterned path, which was contemporary with the building of the cloister range. The path had been constructed using stone roofing tiles from stables or other outbuildings which once stood nearby, or possibly from the original roof of the main house when it was replaced with slate. The archaeological investigation also found the clearly defined indentation of the continuation of the diaper-patterned path, which stretched the whole width of the cloistered garden. (Archaeologists discovered a further cobbled driveway in 1999 leading from the Gatehouse Tower towards the Cloister Garden, its alignment pretty well matching the path in the Cloister Garden.)

The reinstatement of the diaper-patterned path and the surrounding pitched stone cobbling was by far the most laborious task of the whole restoration, with garden staff on their hands and knees for months on end. The closest match to the stone originally used 400 years ago was a riven Pennant sandstone, which was sourced from a quarry near Rhiwfawr, near Swansea. In 2001 it was the

Above: The diaper-patterned path being reinstated in December 2001.

Below: The first section of the surrounding pitched-stone cobbling being laid beside the northern range – only another four months' more work!

last remaining quarry to supply natural stone roofing tiles in South Wales. Sixty tonnes of stone was delivered, out of which around 42,000 individual pieces of stone were selected, most of which had to be split and shaped by hand before being bedded into a base of sand. The surrounding pitched-stone cobbling was sourced locally from a limestone quarry near Porthyrhyd in Carmarthenshire. We hope that the restored pathways will remain in situ for hundreds more years, acting as a testament to the care and dedication of the staff at Aberglasney.

Almost every day, visitors puzzled by the cloisters' appearance ask what the purpose of the deep archways might have been. Several suggestions have been postulated, such as areas for seating, or enclosures for sheltering plants: perhaps they could protect the orange trees from the winter weather. Maybe they had a secondary use, but as demonstrated in classical architecture, an arch is by far the strongest shape to support the walkway and parapet above.

Sadly the cloister range is not complete and nor is it likely to be. The ends of the two wings nearest the house once boasted towers with rooms for resting or banqueting. Although you can see evidence of their existence from scars in the masonry, no

Left: The view along the early seventeenth-century 'cryptoporticus', the cloister-like walk beneath the western range. Historians have compared this to the long gallery in Elizabethan houses, where people could take exercise under cover.

Right: The completed Cloister Garden in spring 2003, planted with period flowers suited to the proverbial 'enamelled mead'.

documentation has come to light which details exactly what their appearance was like, and so they have not been re-created.

Whilst the hard landscaping was dictated by archaeological research, there was no evidence of how the ground plan was laid out, or what style of garden would originally have been made here in the space surrounded by the cloister range.

Advice was sought from Elisabeth Whittle, Cadw's parks and gardens expert, who was convinced that while intricate knot gardens with formally clipped hedges were being created in other parts of Europe, this would not have been the case in west Wales.

Many hours were spent looking through books on garden history to see what style of garden would have been typical during the early part of the seventeenth century in order to create an accurate historical representation. We needed to decide on two points – an appropriate design or pattern for the layout, and what plants to grow in it.

The Dutch polymath Hans Vredeman de Vries designed hundreds of symmetrical grass parterres, illustrated in his book *Hortorum Viridariorumque Formae* published in 1583. It hugely influenced this style of garden design during the late Elizabethan and early Jacobean period. It was the publication of his ideas that disseminated what was to be the

Left: Oranges in lead containers add an exotic fragrance and charm to the Cloister Garden. They are plants that aspiring gardeners of the 1600s like Bishop Rudd and his son Sir Rice would have grown.

Right: Honeysuckle *Lonicera periclymenum* growing on the railings of the flight of steps that leads up to the Parapet Walk.

Previous pages: In the Cloister Garden we use only flowers known in the time of Bishop Rudd and his son Sir Rice, the makers of the original garden, such as the elegant *Tulipa acuminata* (left). The winter aconite *Eranthis hyemalis* (right) is a member of the buttercup family and flowers in late winter and early spring. Compact plants like these make good candidates for including in a flowery mead.

Above: *Crocus flavus* is one of the species known to have been grown in Elizabethan gardens.

Opposite: During the winter months the frost-tender orange trees are replaced by clipped box balls.

vogue of garden design throughout Europe in the early seventeenth century. Another valuable source was a modern book, *The Artist and the Garden* by Roy Strong. This illustrates many paintings of the period, often portraits in which a garden is seen incidentally in the background. Scrutinizing such books is a great source of information for garden historians and restorers. Two paintings from Roy Strong's book influenced our design. The first was a beautiful study of a lady of the Byng family, who lived in Kent, dating from about 1620. The painting shows a window looking out into a cloistered garden surrounding a symmetrical grass parterre. The other painting was a portrait of Sir William Style of Langley, which hangs in the Tate Gallery. Again this shows a cloistered garden with the same kind of formal grassed parterre. It was decided that the garden depicted in the picture of Lady Byng would form the basic layout of the design.

Another complicated decision entailed the planting. Of course, our palette would be restricted to plants known at the period when the garden was first made – the early 1600s. But someone had the idea that we should plant an 'enamelled mead', with 'pinpricks' of flower colour throughout the grassed area. This idealized version of a flowery meadow was another feature of the period, often seen in paintings and tapestries – an alien concept compared to modern trends which favour weed-free 'perfect' lawns.

The reinstatement of the garden within the cloistered area was meticulously researched, even down to the mixture of grass species used to create the parterre. A grass mixture containing a high percentage of fescues was selected, which is commonly found on the less fertile higher ground around Carmarthenshire. The grass is very fine and relatively slow-growing, so therefore, in theory, would not

compete with the cultivated plants within the enamelled mead and would need less frequent mowing than usual lawn varieties.

The planting within the grass was kept very simple, but proved very labour-intensive, as the grass had to be kept low to accentuate the minimalist planting within. In the original gardens many of the plants would have been grown in pots and plunged into the ground when they came into flower and removed and replaced as soon as they went over.

When we first laid out the Cloister Garden, we planted many perennials in the grass, all of them known to have been grown in Britain at the beginning of the seventeenth century. These included *Achillea millefolium*, *Campanula rotundifolia*, several old *Dianthus* cultivars including 'Nonsuch', 'Queen of Sheba' and 'Sops-in-wine', *Scabiosa columbaria* and *Knautia arvensis*, to name just a few. They created limited interest during the summer months, and the maintenance required, with gardeners on their hands and knees clipping the grass around each plant, was far too labour-intensive. To most visitors the result looked like nothing more than a weedy lawn. It was all very well as an idea, but putting it into practice successfully was just not possible.

It was also common practice to use bulbous plants, and as with the perennials, much research was undertaken to source the correct plants which would have been in cultivation during the early seventeenth century. The number of different varieties cultivated at that time was not extensive, but there were some beautiful species which are no longer commonly grown. The season starts with the winter aconite, which flowers from January until March with delicate small yellow flowers, which survive the harsh months of winter without blemish. These are soon followed by *Crocus angustifolius* and

Crocus flavus, *Scilla amoena* and *Scilla hyacinthoides*, and *Muscari comosum*.

Tulipa sylvestris is one of my favourite early spring bulbs and it was used in the re-creation of the Cloister Garden. It is probably a native of Turkey, but has now naturalized from Europe (including Britain) to North Africa and from Asia to Siberia. It is very modest in appearance and its slightly pendulous flower heads have a delicate fragrance, an attribute not usually associated with a tulip. The other tulips that grow in the grass are the short-stemmed *Tulipa schrenkii* and the very distinctive *Tulipa acuminata* with its very long petals.

At the first opportunity after the bulb foliage dies down, the grass is mown to keep the garden looking neat. This planting and maintenance regime works well, enabling us to stage concerts and plays during the summer months. By utilizing the Parapet Walk and the Cloister Garden, a thousand people can be seated in the area.

After the bulbs have finished flowering the grass parterre looks rather uninspiring and downbeat to the uninformed. I know that if the whole area was bedded out with a display of annuals, it would be one of the most photogenic parts of the garden – but that is not what Aberglasney is about.

Apart from the parterre planting, narrow beds were constructed across the top and the bottom of the garden for some ornamental planting, but it was still important to be faithful to using plants of the correct period.

The lavender we chose for the border above the lower retaining wall proved difficult to obtain. So many excellent cultivars have been selected for their colour and compact habit that it took time to find the true *Lavandula angustifolia*, which is native to the Mediterranean and grows waist high. Its wonderful fragrance permeates the cloisters in the summer. Sadly in many modern varieties

scent has been sacrificed for more unusual coloured forms or more compact habit. Ironically, a more compact form would be better in this position as the tall flower spikes of the species tend to mask the view of the cloister range.

The roses planted along the base of the upper retaining wall are *Rosa gallica* var. *officinalis*, also known as the red rose of Lancaster or apothecary's rose. It is of great antiquity, first cultivated during the thirteenth century. It is a showy shrub with erect yet bushy growth and fragrant crimson semi-double flowers in June and July.

There is a temptation to cover walls like these with all sorts of floral treasures, which has recently been the case in the Upper Walled Garden and with the training of fruit on the Lower Walled Garden walls. The Cloister Garden walls, however, are too important to embellish in this way. This is strangely contradictory, as in the seventeenth century it would have been fashionable to have them covered with an evergreen climbing plant, as can been seen in many paintings of similar structures of that period: leaving the stonework exposed would have been considered decidedly crude.

The finishing touch to the design of the Cloister Garden was the addition of the oranges that grow in the lead planters on either side of the garden. There is no evidence that oranges were grown at Aberglasney, but the affluent and influential Rudd family, particularly Bishop Rudd's son, Sir Rice Rudd, who was a favourite in the royal court and moved in elevated circles, would have seen many important gardens. Being able to show off oranges would have suited Sir Rice's 'upwardly mobile' attitude.

Oranges were incorporated in our design when it was discovered that they were probably in cultivation in Wales at St Donat's,

near Cowbridge, by 1594, some forty years after they were first cultivated in England. The two species introduced were *Citrus aurantium* and *Citrus sinensis*, the bitter and the sweet orange. These make a wonderful addition to the garden. Their distinctive fragrance enhances the garden for many months and the fruit are long lasting and highly attractive. The ten orange trees are plunged into lead planters during the frost-free months of the year. The lead planters were made in 2001 to a design typical of the period. During the winter months the oranges are kept in our small frost-free greenhouse and replaced in the garden by clipped box balls.

Smaller planters of the same design were also made to grow the eighteen box balls which are placed underneath the crenellations on the Parapet Walk. The introduction of the box balls on the raised walk is certainly not of any historical authenticity, but a matter of health and safety to prevent people, particularly children, from falling over the edge of the parapet. In today's litigious society the health and safety of visitors has taken precedence over historical integrity and aesthetics.

The raised walk offers some of the finest prospects in the garden, giving elevated views over the Cloister Garden, the Pool Garden and the Upper Walled Garden and views beyond the bounds of the garden to Grongaer Hill and the Tywi valley – not to mention the best seats for viewing performances at concerts and plays.

Opposite: Clipped box balls in lead containers stand against each crenellation in the cloister parapet to prevent children from leaning over the wall. This view over the western Parapet Walk looks beyond the Pool Garden towards some of the old Home Farm buildings.

CHAPTER THREE

THE OLD WALLED GARDENS

These walled enclosures were once productive kitchen gardens in the days when estates like Aberglasney would have been self-sufficient. Old Ordnance Survey maps show the former pattern of paths and beds – the basic cruciform layout with perimeter paths was a style repeated in modest country-house gardens everywhere. The kitchen gardens were functional, but also decorative, perhaps with flowers for cutting and espaliered fruit trees; all of the walls would have been productive.

It is a misconception that walled gardens were originally built to protect the garden from the worst of the weather: they can actually be colder. Their main function was the security of the crops, not only protecting them from wildlife, but more importantly keeping the valuable produce from being stolen. Often a gardener was housed within the walled garden, principally for night security. The other main benefit is the heat-retaining properties of the south- and west-facing walls, which advance the ripening of the long-awaited produce. The walls acted as a brilliant support for training the fruit.

Previous pages: Geometry is well suited to a rectangular walled enclosure. The pristine box hedges create the framework for the informal herbaceous planting within the borders.

Left: Spring flowers are the delight of both ornamental and productive gardens: soaring spikes of *Camassia leichtlinii* 'Semiplena' in the Upper Walled Garden.

Right: The single pure white flowers and golden anthers of the crab apple *Malus sargentii* trained on the fruit arch in the Lower garden.

Together with the Cloister Garden, these two walled rectangles form the core of the formal gardens. Someone once suggested that Aberglasney has a greater square footage of wall in relation to ground space than any other garden. I have not checked this by measuring, but it often feels as if it could be true. Now that we garden for pleasure rather than for produce, our walls play a vital part in the garden's design. Aesthetically, walls make a stunning backdrop to ornamental plants. Walls also conceal, so play an important role in a garden's dynamics. Their doorways and openings offer glimpses of other areas beyond, providing visitors with that essential incitement to explore.

THE UPPER WALLED GARDEN

Like the rest of the garden, this area was uncultivated for something like half a century and totally overgrown. Rumour has it that it was ploughed up to plant potatoes sometime around the 1960s, effectively obliterating any traces of the former path system visible on the Ordnance Survey maps. The site originally had a much greater slope than it does today, giving better drainage and light penetration to the crops, but the new ornamental layout commanded a more level platform to work from.

Left: The colourful array of flowers, fruit and vegetables in the Lower Walled Garden is enticing when seen from above through the adjoining doorway.

Right: The theory that a framework of clipped evergreens provides all-year structure is proved by this winter picture of the Upper Walled Garden.

Only two plants remained, one fallen apple tree near the lower wall, and an interesting fig tree. This was once planted against the west-facing wall, but over time the branches rubbed against the stone wall and eventually took root. The trunk has since died, but the fig tree continues to grow well and bears lovely fruit from its impoverished lodging, which is exactly how they like it. I inform as many people as I can that the fruits of this particular fig are poisonous and cause extreme stomach cramps and convulsions. I must say it convincingly, as quite a few visitors believe me – there is nothing quite like a fresh ripe fig!

In 1997, well before serious restoration was under way, Penelope Hobhouse, one of the country's most eminent garden designers, was asked to create a new design for this walled garden. The formality of the layout reflects Aberglasney's historic past, and Penelope Hobhouse drew for inspiration on a seventeenth-century design. The principal feature is the central path system, which is laid out in the form of a Celtic cross. This also echoes the nineteenth-century pattern of cruciform paths in the traditional kitchen

Left: Early autumn, looking diagonally across the Upper Walled Garden to the west façade of the mansion. The Cloister Garden is beyond the wall on the left.

Right, above: The back-lit flowers of *Wisteria sinensis* 'Alba' hanging above an opening into the Upper Walled Garden.

Right, below: Like the 94-carat diamond with the same name, *Crocosmia* x *crocosmiiflora* 'Star of the East' is a jewel among montbretias. Orange is a difficult colour to place in a garden, but the silver-grey foliage of *Euphorbia characias* subsp. *wulfenii* makes a good foil.

garden layout and makes use of the principal doorways into the garden. It suits a rectangular garden like this to have a geometric layout and, as with the adjoining Cloister Garden, you have access to wonderful elevated vantage points from the walkways. The best bird's-eye view of the Upper Walled Garden is looking south from the Cloister Garden walkway; irrespective of the season, the view never fails to impress the visitor. The concentric box-edged beds are beautiful during every season.

As you stroll through the garden at ground level the oblique visual impression is quite a different experience. You are able to encounter plants face-to-face and the curving paths entice you to walk between and around the enclosed box-edged beds to explore the diversity within.

The herbaceous plants used within the eight beds are far from historic; it is the amalgamation of the non-contemporary elements that elevates this garden into another sphere. Many of the original plants used in Penelope Hobhouse's design still

Above left: All traces of the original layout were obliterated in the 1960s, when potatoes were grown here. The neglected garden, like the overgrown wood beyond, could be treated as a blank canvas for a fresh planting scheme.

Below left: Penelope Hobhouse's design combining concentric ellipses with a cruciform path layout takes shape in the early summer of 1999 – just weeks before Aberglasney opened.

Right: Late summer with *Eupatorium purpureum* subsp. *maculatum* 'Atropurpureum' and the perennial sunflower *Helianthus* 'Lemon Queen' making an impressive stately display.

thrive. Her original choice of herbaceous plants was a deliberate, anachronistic celebration of what's available today. Tall, head-high herbaceous plants such as eupatorium, helianthus, helenium and thalictrum create a wonderful intimacy by constricting the outer view. Long-lasting flowers such as *Anaphalis triplinervis* 'Sommerschnee' and *Nepeta* 'Six Hills Giant' are attractive throughout the summer and autumn (the nepeta is best cut back after flowering to keep it compact and repeat-flowering). Also valuable are flowers that come out in succession, like hemerocallis (the day-lily). It is hard to keep up with the day-lilies. There are well over twenty thousand registered cultivars, and this

Left: The northwest corner of the Upper Walled Garden looking over the Pool Garden, its wall red with Boston ivy, towards the holiday cottages in the former farm.

Right: The brilliant autumn colour of *Lagerstroemia indica* 'Petite Pinkie', a rare cultivar of the crape myrtle, planted in the favourable aspect of the south-facing wall.

Following pages: The sensory appeal of perennials includes not only the obvious sight and scent, but also movement. The large scented panicles of *Escallonia bifida* (far left) must attract more butterflies and bees than any other plant in the garden. The fragrant flowers of *Hemerocallis citrina* open in the afternoon and are at their peak at night. *Pennisetum alopecuroides* 'Hameln' is one of the few grasses we grow for its feathery flower heads and its autumn colour. *Anemone* x *hybrida* 'Honorine Jobert' is a particularly choice cultivar. The elegant pure white flowers are produced on wiry, branched stems from August to October and can continue to flower even after a light frost.

remarkable figure is increasing by up to eight hundred new named cultivars each year. The genus is native to China, where parts of the plant are eaten as a vegetable; they contain high quantities of Vitamin C. Here at Aberglasney we grow the delicate yellow *Hemerocallis citrina*.

The shapely flower heads of umbellifers add their distinctive silhouettes to the beds, often lasting as seed heads on into winter. I find *Selinum wallichianum* quite magical, as did the plant connoisseur E.A. Bowles. He described it as 'the queen of all umbellifers, with its almost transparent tender green-ness and the marvellously lacy pattern of its large leaves, the most beautiful of all fern-leaved plants.'

The clipped conical yews are superb at providing firm structure during the winter

Opposite: Perennials have infinite variety, whether grouped in a border composition or examined in close-up, in colourful flower or as crisp seed heads. The spring combination includes camassia, nepeta, geranium, alchemilla, lysimachia and *Iris sibirica*.

Above: A perfectly formed flower head of fennel, encrusted with frost.

Following pages: As well as combining in stunning colour compositions, perennials offer their flowers for detailed examination. Far left: The purple single flowers of *Thalictrum rochebrunianum* (above). A bulbous plant related to the hyacinth, the double *Camassia leichtlinii* 'Semiplena' (below) flowers in spring. Centre: The magical *Selinum wallichianum* illuminated by early morning sun. Right: The fringed beauty of *Geranium phaeum* var. *phaeum* 'Samobor'.

months, but evergreen shrubs like *Phlomis fruticosa* or sub-shrubs such as *Euphorbia characias* subsp. *wulfenii* 'Lambrook Gold' with a softer silhouette are also valuable. The silver-grey leaves of this dramatic euphorbia serve as a foil to bright colours such as the long, clear orange flowers of the stunning montbretia *Crocosmia* x *crocosmiiflora* 'Star of the East'. Held horizontally on branching stems, these make a glorious display from late summer to mid autumn.

Some perennials also have dramatic foliage; *Cynara cardunculus* is one of the most striking, and this is a good site for grasses like *Pennisetum alopecuroides* 'Hameln'. Not many grasses are grown in Aberglasney's borders and beds, but this variety of foxtail grass, also commonly called fountain grass, is an exception. The flowers appear from midsummer and persist well into the autumn, when the leaves turn an attractive ochre.

I am glad not to be dealing with one of those faithful reproductions of a planting by someone like Gertrude Jekyll, based on one of her famous original plans. Whilst it is educational to see authentic Gertrude Jekyll borders replicated with bona-fide cultivars, I don't believe they should be perpetuated ad infinitum. I believe that the planting of a garden should not stay static and stagnate. The principles of good garden design remain the same, but new species and different and superior forms are constantly appearing, offering new planting possibilities. Good designers appreciate the constant tweaking of a design rather than have it eternally set in aspic.

In the spring, before the bolder colours of the flowers, there is a magical moment when the fresh emerging herbaceous foliage contrasting with the solid-looking fresh green new growth of the clipped box creates one of

those supremely pleasing visual effects, proving that form, texture – and colour – are the essential ingredients in a good composition. This was Penelope Hobhouse's principle: a strong permanent structure with ephemeral decorative infilling.

The central feature designed by Penelope Hobhouse dominates the ground plan, but plants are gradually creeping in and colonizing the margins of the garden, too. A bed at the foot of the south-facing wall was planted in 1999 soon after the garden opened. Selections of tender bulbous and woody plants were chosen to benefit from the warm sheltered position. These included a collection of different agapanthus including *Agapanthus campanulatus* 'Oxford Blue',

Agapanthus 'Bressingham Blue', the more tender *Agapanthus africanus* and *Tulbaghia violacea*, which emanates a strong garlicky smell, which is particularly pungent during the autumn and winter when the foliage dies down. For this reason it is best ostracized to a place away from the house. Another striking plant here is the Chilean *Lobelia tupa*, grown for its beautifully felted leaves and narrow tubular red flowers in late summer. Its common name is devil's tobacco, as the leaves are said to be hallucinogenic when smoked. There is such an incredible range of plants available. I have a strong aversion to trying to grow plants that are known to be too tender to survive our moderately mild winters and having to cosset them by covering them up for the winter.

Above left: *Thalictrum delavayi* 'Hewitt's Double', commonly known as double meadow rue, has beautiful, lacy foliage like a small form of maidenhair fern. The cloud-like sprays of double pink flowers are also outstanding for cutting.

Above: *Phlomis fruticosa*, or Jerusalem sage, comes from the Mediterranean region. It belongs to the family Lamiaceae, which includes many culinary herbs, but this is purely ornamental.

Opposite: *Agapanthus campanulatus* 'Oxford Blue' and *Agapanthus* 'Bressingham Blue' with *Tulbaghia violacea*, a member of the onion family, growing in the warm south-facing border. The ancient fig tree is on the right of the archway.

Along the wall several less hardy shrubs were selected, including *Lagerstroemia indica* 'Petite Pinkie', a rarely seen cultivar of the crape myrtle purchased in 1989 from Otto Eisenhut's nursery situated above lake Maggiore in Switzerland. It is a plant of many attributes; it has lovely cinnamon-coloured bark, plumes of pink flowers in late summer and brilliant autumn colour. *Escallonia bifida* from southern Brazil and Uruguay is another beautiful rare shrub grown against the wall. It attracts a wide range of butterflies in late summer; in fact it probably attracts more butterflies than any other plant in the garden. It is slightly tender and benefits from wall protection.

Other plants include species of *Prostanthera*, *Leptospermum*, *Banksia*, *Grevillea* and *Correa*, all from Australasia. I have also planted one of my favourite trees: it was called *Michelia doltsopa* at the time, but it has recently been absorbed into the genus *Magnolia*. It was introduced to Britain from Tibet by the famous plant collector George Forrest in about 1918. This evergreen species is seen at its best when grown in more sheltered gardens, particularly in the warmer gardens in Cornwall. I planted it here in 1999 and in 2009, to my great delight, it produced its first flower.

Another tender plant which has matured well is an olive, which was purchased from a specialist grower who sold it as 'The Chelsea Physic Garden Hardy Form'. It has survived here in a sheltered niche for nine years. The original plant at the Chelsea Physic Garden was probably planted just before the Second World War and thrives in the London microclimate. More recently new olive cultivars have been bred which are reputedly even hardier; it will be interesting to hear how they perform.

The original design excluded the planting

of the north, west and east-facing walls, with the intention of making the central design more prominent. The temptation to utilize the walls was too great for me and in 2008 a path was laid around the garden to give access to the walls, which can now finally be clothed with trained plants. A collection of figs is grown on the west-facing wall and rare climbers such as *Holboellia*, *Stauntonia* and *Bomarea* are grown on the north- and east-facing walls.

Opposite: What E.A. Bowles called 'the almost transparent tender green-ness of *Selinum wallichianum*'.

Above: The Chilean *Lobelia tupa* flourishes in a wall bed in the warm southwest corner, flowering in mid to late summer.

THE LOWER WALLED GARDEN

Above: Apples and pears are trained against the west-facing wall in the form of a 'Belgian Fence', an attractive criss-cross espalier technique not often seen in Britain.

Opposite: Walls were built to protect garden crops from unwelcome intruders. The Lower Walled Garden seen from the northwest, with the Pool Garden and Meadow in the foreground, and farmland beyond.

Following pages: The crab apple tunnel runs the length of the Lower Walled Garden, straddling the path alongside the west wall, and is particularly beautiful in spring and in autumn. The fruits of Sargent's crab (*Malus sargentii*) are of ornamental rather than culinary value.

This is the area of the garden where the cultivation of fruit, vegetables and flowers takes place. When the garden was cleared, like the Upper Walled Garden it had one remaining apple tree, which despite having a hollow trunk still stands, but unfortunately produces a very second-rate fruit.

Because there was no special archaeological interest in this enclosure to rival that nearer the house, this was the first garden that could be laid out and planted. Just before I arrived the four main planting beds had been outlined in dwarf box. Annuals were sown in the spring of 1999 to give some colour to the garden. You could hear early visitors give a sigh of relief when they reached this area and saw some flowers, albeit just a few rows of annuals, but at the time it was like an oasis in a muddy desert.

It was strange to find that the garden consisted of only three walls: the south-facing wall, the one that is the most important for the cultivation of more tender fruit, was missing. It was only after investigating old Ordnance Survey maps that it was discovered that a wall did once exist. This was confirmed when archaeologists undertook a survey and found evidence of part of a wall buried a metre or so below the surface. The wall was duly rebuilt, giving the opportunity of planting a range of stone fruit including apricots, nectarines and peaches, which have been espaliered against the wall.

The high west-facing wall backing the Upper Walled Garden has been planted with espaliered apples and pears trained in the form of a 'Belgian Fence' – a sophisticated scheme creating a diagonal grid of branches

on the wall that is not uncommon in Europe. This is best achieved by selecting young grafted trees with a double leader, which is not usually desirable: you may have to ask the nurseryman to create them specially. Alternatively, you can buy a maiden with a single stem and cut it back to the desired height – making sure you have two opposite buds, which can then be trained. The inspiration came from Frank Cabot, who showed me a picture of his Belgian Fence growing in one of his gardens. This unusual feature is now much admired.

The art of creating espalier fruit trees is not usually thought to be an ancient horticultural practice, but one pursued by the haute bourgeoisie of the Victorian gardening fraternity. This could not be further from the truth; pruning fruit tree branches into shaped forms has a time-honoured place in the history of gardening. Egyptian tomb paintings of around 1400 BC reflect images of espaliered fig trees growing in the Pharaoh's garden. In medieval times, European monks carefully trained fruit and nut trees to grow flat against the walls of great monastic gardens. During the seventeenth century in England, and especially in France, espalier-trained fruit gained widespread popularity, appearing on humble village walls as well as in elaborate

Above left: Empty beds prepared for planting in 1999, with the Pool Garden visible in the background. Two years later the missing south-facing wall separating the gardens was rebuilt following archaeological evidence.

Left: Flowers and vegetables in full production, with the Loggia in the background.

Opposite: A crop of much-admired sweet peas for cutting is grown every year.

configurations in the Versailles kitchen garden of Louis XIV. When Victorian head gardeners showed off their skills in this department (as the proliferation of old nails found in the walls proves they did at Aberglasney), they were following a long-standing practice.

During every month of the year, espaliered plants create an attractive symmetry and an example of living architecture. They have the added benefit of producing more abundant flowers and fruit because the strict summer-pruning regime (also known as the Lorette system) encourages the formation of flowering buds. In pursuit of year-round self-sufficiency, the old gardeners would have trained fruit on both sides of the walls. Ripening could be brought forward on a sunny aspect with the aid of protection against late frosts, while fruit grown on the shadier outer walls would ripen later and extend the season.

Apples have been grown in Wales for many centuries. The patron saint of fruit trees is St Teilo, a contemporary of St David who was born around AD 500. He has local connections, being based (and possibly buried) in the nearby town of Llandeilo, to which he gave his name. He would have almost certainly travelled along the Roman road which passes near where Aberglasney now stands.

One of the very few fragments of historical record relating to Aberglasney's gardens is a notebook belonging to one of the eighteenth-century Dyers, who listed the apples he planted here (though we're not sure exactly where). It included numbers of 'Paradise', 'Golden and Royal Russetings', 'Pearmain', 'Orange Pippin' and 'Non Pareil'. Today several Welsh varieties are espaliered on the wall, including Cissy, Glansevin, Drith Mawr, Pen Caled, Pen Glas and Pig Aderyn. All were purchased from a local nursery in nearby

Capel Isaac that specializes in Welsh varieties. There is a resurgence of interest in local varieties of fruit throughout Britain, and an astonishing 1000 different apple trees are available from specialist nurseries around the country. Our apples at Aberglasney have all been grafted on to dwarfing rootstocks to contain their vigour.

The lower north-facing wall has been planted with blackberries and blackcurrants with blueberries planted in the bed below and the east-facing wall with raspberries and loganberries.

One of the most attractive features in the garden is an arch formed using *Malus sargentii*, Sargent's crab apple. Charles Sargent, who collected seeds of this species along with 200 other plants on a trip to Japan in 1892, introduced this beautiful tree to Britain. The archway runs the length of the garden – like a tunnel – and is clothed in spring with pure white flowers with contrasting golden anthers. These are followed by small, bright red, cherry-like fruits in late summer, which stay on until late autumn.

Cutting flowers were traditionally grown in country-house gardens. The two beds used for cut flowers are the most brightly coloured and eye-catching part of the garden, and for that reason it is often the most admired. A wide variety of different annuals is grown from seed each year, selected for their ability

Left: Swiss chard, a hardy beet, comes in a range of colours. Besides being highly ornamental, it is a useful culinary plant, with edible leaf stalks and leaves.

Right: Four box-edged beds divide the garden into the traditional quartered layout. The unnamed apple tree at the centre is a relic of the past, but the quality of its fruit leaves a lot to be desired.

Right: Late summer with a kaleidoscope of colour from the cutting border.

Following pages: The charming, delicately fragrant flowers of *Gladiolus murielae* (top left and centre) are a great addition to the cut-flower garden. Borage (bottom left) not only provides the decoration for Pimms' but is rich in gamma linoleic acid, active against some cancers. The striking seed heads of *Scabiosa* 'Paper Moon' (right) are aptly named.

to keep in a vase once picked, and these are used in the cottages, meeting rooms, offices, café and the lavatories.

In an exit survey undertaken in 2007, the sweet pea was the most popular flower in the garden, which is understandable, but considering some of the cherished plants in the garden I find a little disappointing. Other top performers are helichrysum, which looks good fresh and dried, salvia (clary), cornflower, asters – a good flower for harvest festivals, *Acidanthera murielae* (now known as *Gladiolus murielae*) and *Ammi majus* (the bishop's flower), which is like a delicate miniature cow parsley and, like florists' gypsophylla, compliments any arrangement.

Scabiosa atropurpurea and the cultivar 'Paper Moon', which has soft lavender flowers, is not particularly stunning in a border, but when cut the seed heads are very attractive and much admired by flower arrangers. Statice, also known as limonium or sea lavender, is another plant that is very useful for dried arrangements. A plant that is always admired is *Cerinthe major* 'Purpurascens', the honeywort that has glaucous green leaves and deep purple-bell flowers, which are adored by bees.

The two vegetable beds furnish the topic of many a conversation. Until you work in a garden that is open to the public, you do not realize how many 'experts' are more than willing to offer advice and quite a bit of criticism. It seems that everyone has their own tried and tested method, which produces vegetables of superior quality. Occasionally we do get it right and the

The bright patch of colour beyond the box-edged path is *Amaranthus caudatus* or love-lies-bleeding. Its trailing flower spikes resembling chenille make this a remarkable – and unusual – cut flower.

complimentary comments are a welcome relief. One positive comment is how colourful the vegetable garden is, from the bright colours of the chard through to the deep purples of cabbage, but the most dramatic are the various coloured lettuces, grown in succession in regimented rows.

It is very satisfying seeing the kitchen staff walk to the Lower Walled Garden in the morning during the summer and return with collection of freshly gathered herbs in a trug. We are often asked whether we should not try to maximize vegetable production and supply the Aberglasney café? Should we try to grow vegetables worthy of a show bench, or should it be our mission to inspire visitors and encourage them to grow their own vegetables at home? It would be nice to be able do all these things, but in fact we use this principally as a show garden. We do use some of the vegetables at home and in the end very little is wasted, because anything left over is either dug in as a green manure or composted.

I am often surprised by people's perception that only supermarkets seem to be able to supply winter vegetables. We don't 'clamp' any vegetables for winter use, but leave what we can in the ground to harvest when needed. True, the outer cabbage leaves may look unappetizing, but when removed they reveal fine fresh specimens.

The ornamental border below the Belgian Fence has been planted for summer and autumn interest with many different asters including the majestic aster relative *Achillea grandiflora*, with its large flat heads of creamy white flowers. We also grow the white *Sidalcea candida* and the beautiful pink form 'Elsie Heugh'. An impressive plant for the back of the border is the brassica relative *Crambe cordifolia*, with sprays of small white flowers that look like an erupting gypsophila. With the herbaceous plants cut down at the

beginning of winter, the border looks barren, but this allows the striking architectural framework of the Belgian Fence to dominate.

A recent addition in the southeast corner of the Lower Walled Garden is the Loggia, which now acts as a focal point at the end of the long path that runs along the top of this garden. It was built in 2007 after a generous donation had been given to the Trust by a garden visitor from the north of England who said that Aberglasney was the nicest garden she had ever visited and on her first visit in 2004 gave the Restoration Trust some money to plant a tree. Thankfully the tree, the lovely *Tilia henryana* planted near the Gatehouse, has grown well.

The slate roof of the Loggia is unusual in being constructed from a reclaimed pale buff slate, which was once quarried from Maenclochog on the Pembrokeshire–Carmarthenshire border. Such an elaborate structure would not have traditionally been built in a 'working garden'; such comforts would most certainly not have been afforded for the hard-working gardeners of the past, but it is now a much-needed retreat for garden visitors. This is one example of the way the garden 'grows' and moves with the times. The fact that a visitor feels inspired to make a gift like this is particularly gratifying. The donor of the Loggia is now elderly and seldom visits, but I know she is pleased to have a presence in the garden in this way.

Opposite: Bamboo canes support spiders' webs in early autumn.

Above: The Loggia provides a focal point at the end of the path along the top of the garden, between standard bay trees on the right and the high west-facing wall on the left.

CHAPTER FOUR

THE HILL ABOVE THE HOUSE

To build the original Aberglasney mansion, a portion of the naturally sloping ground was quarried out and levelled to reach bedrock foundations. As a result the building sits tucked well into the hillside, with only narrow passageways behind it to the east and south. On the opposite sides of the house, more open ground with a modest gradient provided the opportunity to make the formal gardens that were fashionable in both the Rudds' time and during the nineteenth century. The steeper rising ground behind the house presents an entirely different gardening landscape, where formality is not possible. Apart from a centuries-old path running uphill to the parish church, and some Victorian remnants – evergreens, and some aviaries – the area was 'terra incognita'. I could not have wished for it to be more perfect: it had all the ingredients necessary to create a beautiful woodland garden.

Gradually the area has developed different garden identities, with different planting themes. This is definitely an area to explore,

Previous pages: The charming *Lilium mackliniae*, discovered around fifty years ago in Manipur, northeast India.

Left: The collection of trees grown for their colour on the slope near the mansion includes *Nyssa sinensis*, *Nyssa sylvatica*, *Cornus* 'Ormonde' and *Cornus* 'Eddie's White Wonder'.

Right: *Matteuccia struthiopteris*, the shuttlecock or ostrich fern, emerging in the spring below the bridge, with the tree fern *Dicksonia antarctica* in the background.

with no set route prescribed. You invariably approach from somewhere near the mansion, whether you head off uphill or follow the level path above the Upper Walled Gardens past the Aviaries. The areas merge into one another, but we can single out a handful of distinctive 'gardens', each with a different atmosphere.

BISHOP RUDD'S WALK

This part of the garden was given its name because Bishop Rudd, who purchased Aberglasney around 1600, would have regularly used this path to walk up to St Cathen's church. Over the centuries other successive occupants of Aberglasney would have followed in his footsteps as they went to worship in the parish church.

Bishop Rudd's Walk was once probably quite an interesting part of the garden. Somewhere in the archives among the references to this area of Aberglasney is the term 'American Garden' – a garden style dating from the late eighteenth century, when 'informal' shrubby plantings of prized acid-loving evergreens newly introduced from North America became fashionable. The style persisted into Victorian times with the addition of evergreen plants from other continents, and the tangled laurels and rhododendrons were probably vestiges of that era, having shaded out other less vigorous companions.

By the 1990s, most of the slope above the house epitomized people's idea of the neglect and gloom typical of an overgrown Victorian estate, probably untouched for most

Bishop Rudd's Walk in the late spring of 2003, three years after it was planted.

of the twentieth century. The original plantings of rhododendrons and laurels had grown and spread into an impenetrable mass of twisting branches, augmented by drawn seedling trees. From the first time I encountered this part of the garden, I knew this area could have the potential of being the most exciting area of botanical interest.

To the uninitiated it may have looked dank and discouraging, but to me it was such a welcome opportunity. The years of neglect had created a humus rich soil, with a thick covering of well decomposed leaf litter free of unwanted pernicious weed. This was in stark contrast to other, flatter parts of the garden, where the ground had been compacted by heavy machinery that had ruined the soil structure, rendering it useless.

Clearance work started in the winter of 1999, when the tangled scrub and seedling ash trees were removed. Oaks, yews and spruce were retained. The work had to be undertaken very sensitively as the whole of the grounds of Aberglasney are within a Conservation Area. Regular meetings took place with Carmarthenshire County Council's Conservation Officers who scrutinized the progress and checked that strict adherence to the authorized planning consents was maintained.

The task was made more onerous by my belief in thorough preparation. Not only did weed trees have to be cut down, but all their roots had to be removed for fear of the area becoming infested with honey fungus. A constantly perpetuated fallacy is that honey fungus will only attack weak plants. There are actually three different species of honey fungus in the UK, two of which are potentially lethal to plants. Specimens that are weak are certainly more prone to attack, but I have known vigorously growing plants succumb to it as well.

For this reason all stumps from felled trees in the garden are removed to ensure that they don't become host to this clandestine killer. It is a costly and time-consuming task, but nothing can be more frustrating than seeing one of your coveted plants perish to this fungal infection. We used a small garden tractor to which a small hydraulic backhoe was added to remove the stumps. This has proved to be one of the most useful pieces of equipment purchased for the garden.

After the site was cleared it revealed an attractive valley with a gentle ravine and a meandering little stream. It couldn't have been more perfect – dappled shade, moisture and an open, slightly acidic soil, perfect for the selection of rarely seen woodland treasures I wanted to cultivate.

The area was landscaped, with the planting areas interlaced by an enticing network of paths, allowing people to wander about the area and to study the plants at close quarters. The steep slopes were made more accessible by creating rustic steps using oak risers. An attractive arching oak bridge across the ravine allowed greater visual access to the stream and planting below. I managed to source 40 tonnes of coniferous leaf-litter from a mature clear-felled forestry plantation, which was dug in as additional moisture-retentive organic matter.

In the areas that had not been smothered by rampant light-excluding vegetation, it was important to keep the attractive and diverse native flora, which complimented the newly introduced plants. There was already a good population of indigenous spring-flowering plants, including violets, wood

Above: Clearing scrub and tree roots in Bishop Rudd's Walk in 1999.

Opposite: The giant lily *Cardiocrinum giganteum* towering above emerging rodgersia leaves.

anemones, primroses and blankets of *Adoxa moschatellina*, better known as townhall clock (because the plant has flowers on four sides). These natives were augmented by other spring-flowering plants, including several small-cupped narcissus, which look as if they have always been there. As with tulips, it is the smaller daffodils of delicate, modest stature that I prefer – they don't have to be old varieties or pure species, as some newer hybrids can also possess those desirable qualities. It is also nice when a plant has a story behind it – like the lovely long-flowering *Narcissus* 'Cedric Morris'. Sir Cedric Morris spent his childhood around Swansea and is best known for his works of art. He was also a fanatical plant collector and his gardening friend Beth Chatto named this daffodil posthumously after him.

Before choosing the herbaceous plants for a woodland setting, it is important to deal

Left: The wonderful native flora of wild primroses and violets is a great asset to inherit. The area must be carefully managed to ensure its continued survival.

Right: *Narcissus* 'Verger' is a lovely small-cupped cultivar for naturalizing – its simplicity and understatement are great virtues.

Following pages, left: The dainty *Narcissus* 'Cedric Morris' is a treasure to have in the garden. It is one of the first daffodils to flower, often as early as late November, and continues to flower until March.

Following pages, right: Among our shrubby plants, forms and cultivars of *Daphne bholua* such as the scented 'Jacqueline Postill' are a great attraction. This superb seedling raised from the cultivar 'Peter Smithers' is named 'Limpsfield' and has particularly dark flowers.

with the larger woody plants first, by removing any unsuitable specimens and replanting with choice varieties. These not only provide structure and interest, but are very necessary to create the dappled shade many woodland herbaceous plants enjoy.

Given the woodland setting – and my personal fascination with the genus – the first woody specimens to be introduced to this area were magnolias. It was a selection of the large Asiatic magnolias that I chose to plant here, namely *Magnolia sprengeri* 'Wakehurst', *Magnolia* 'Philip Tregunna', *Magnolia* 'Harold Hillier' and *Magnolia* 'Albatross'. Not only are they some of the most beautiful available, but I wanted to grow them because I acquired a sentimental attachment to all of them in my previous positions, either because I knew the people they were named after or for the wonderful memories of the gardens they grew in. These magnolias and all the other semi-mature specimen magnolias at Aberglasney were grafted in 1993 and moved with me to Aberglasney in 1999.

There should always be something of interest to see and to smell, and daphnes are an obvious choice. One of the most admired groups is the clump of *Daphne bholua* 'Jacqueline Postill' at the start of the ascent up the path. It starts to flower in December and continues through to March, filling the air with its intoxicating, addictive fragrance. Another group of this daphne is situated at the top of the path, allowing one to indulge in its heavenly fragrance once more. There are now several named forms available. In its native habitat of Nepal and Bhutan, it grows in thickets and pastureland. It is variable in leaf: the higher the elevation the more deciduous the species becomes. Most of the plants available are either micropropagated, grafted or sown from imported seed. I have

never seen ripe seed on any plants grown in the UK, although in warmer climates it can seed itself so much as to become 'a free-seeding exotic'. Some green-fingered propagators have reputedly been able to root plants from cuttings, which is something I have dismally failed at despite several attempts in the past. Until recently the darkest coloured form was a cultivar named after Peter Smithers, who collected the seeds in 1970 from Daman Ridge in Nepal at about 9,000 feet. This has now been superseded by a superb seedling raised from the cultivar 'Peter Smithers' which is named 'Limpsfield' and is available from specialist nurseries.

Above: The first group of hardy exotic orchids to be planted at Aberglasney was *Cypripedium parviflorum* var. *pubescens*. They have flourished and flowered well and have become one of the highlights of the year.

Left: *Cypripedium reginae* is known as the showy lady's slipper orchid. It is certainly one of the most beautiful. The white and pink flowers are more exotic-looking than most hardy species. They are very slow to increase, but the reward for good culture is breathtaking.

In the damp oceanic climate of west Wales moisture-loving fern varieties, both native and exotic, do very well. Ferns are such a varied, useful and obliging group of plants, but they are often taken for granted – perhaps especially here, where they grow so abundantly. The first ferns we introduced to Bishop Rudd's Walk were some large tree ferns, *Dicksonia antarctica*, which relish the damp shady atmosphere and grow totally unprotected from the cold winter weather. On rare occasions when temperatures have dropped to double figures, the fronds have gone brown, but new fronds appear in the spring. To look down from the wooden bridge

into the massive two-metre fronds is a wonderful sight. The tree ferns have since been complimented by a wide range of other terrestrial ferns, which add interest, soften the woodland floor and create a backcloth to the more prominent plants.

Blechnum chilense makes a dramatic display with its large evergreen fronds at the top of Bishop Rudd's Walk. It is a stout evergreen fern with dark bold foliage and spreads easily by rhizomes. Most years it is perfectly hardy, but it can be susceptible to damage during very cold winters. An exciting new introduction is *Blechnum magellanicum* from the wet and cold rainforests of extreme

southern Chile. In its native habitat it develops a trunk and when mature looks very much like a cycad. I spotted one for sale at a nursery in the Severn valley, which always has a collection of desirables. I succumbed to temptation and bought a young (but expensive) specimen and planted it in 2008 at the top of Bishop Rudd's walk. During the cold winter of 2008/2009 I was sure this new treasure would perish, but it actually proved to be hardier than the *Blechnum chilense* that grows nearby.

I also find the delicate, finer-leaved species attractive, including the various forms of *Adiantum pedatum* and *Adiantum aleuticum*. The most remarkably coloured fronds must be those of *Athyrium niponicum* var. *pictum* 'Red Beauty', also known as the Japanese painted lady fern, and *Dryopteris erythrosora*, another colourful fern that has bright red new fronds in the spring.

By the end of March, there is much in flower among the herbaceous plants. The first dog's-tooth violet to flower is *Erythronium dens-canis*, a very dwarf-growing species which is very welcome, but its impact does not compare to the later-flowering forms such as 'White Splendour' and 'Pagoda' (which is also naturalizing in Pigeon House Wood).

This part of the garden is particularly beautiful in the spring and early summer – the season when woodland flora is most exuberant and most welcome. Later come lilies and a range of more unusual herbaceous plants like kirengeshoma, tricyrtis and actaea.

Various herbaceous genera such as

Left: A spider's web with the first ray of morning sun gracing the native lady fern *Athyrium filix-femina*.

Right: *Onoclea sensibilis* is commonly known as the sensitive fern – not that it is difficult to cultivate, but it dies down at the first sign of frost.

hellebores and epimediums are both woodland treasures and woodland stalwarts, contributing greatly to the 'furnishing' of the humus-rich ground beneath the tree and shrub canopy. We grow a good range of primulas, exotic relatives of our native primroses, which self-seed in our moist soil and spread into generous carpets, contributing great splashes of colour. A number of different species of trilliums – members of the Trilliaceae – seem to do exceptionally well in the humus-rich soil in this area and their shapely forms make attractive clumps in bare soil. Visitors are also intrigued by introductions – related to our arums – in the genus *Arisaema*, tuberous-rooted plants grown as much for their beautiful architectural leaves as their unusual striped hooded spathes. Some of these do not emerge from the soil to flower until June, so can be easily damaged by unknowing feet – one of the reasons I deplore seeing visitors treading on cultivated areas of the garden, and don't hesitate to reprimand them.

The most exquisitely beautiful of all the herbaceous woodland plants has to be the blue Himalayan poppy *Meconopsis grandis*, and to come across a great drift of these iridescent blue flowers is an inspiring sight. But they and their other Asiatic poppy relatives are quite a challenge to keep going (the exception is *Meconopsis cambrica*, the Welsh poppy, which can become a highly invasive weed) and although we should have just the right conditions, we have to work hard at Aberglasney to maintain the impression that they are naturalizing without assistance in the landscape.

Another coveted plant here is *Glaucidium palmatum* var. *leucanthum*, the white form of the Japanese wood poppy. It is one of Japan's most beautiful woodland plants. It can be difficult to grow; in A. T. Johnson's book *A*

Woodland Garden, published in 1937, he wrote of the species: 'It has been accorded all the ceremony its price and persuasion merits, yet it likes us not.' So far the plants at Aberglasney are growing well. It is closely related to the buttercup family, but distinct enough to be placed in its own family, the Glaucidiaceae.

If *Meconopsis* are the most beautiful herbaceous plants, *Nomocharis* must be the most exquisite of bulbous plants. Twenty years ago, I recall seeing a coloured plate illustrating *Nomocharis mairei* in *Lilies*, written by Patrick M. Synge. This book was a revision of a monumental work produced towards the end of the nineteenth century by H. J. Elwes entitled *A Monograph of the Genus Lilium*. In this publication a series of magnificent plates represented all the lilies at that time in cultivation in Great Britain, the drawings made from living specimens. I was curious to know more about this unknown lily relative.

The Yorkshire plant hunter Reginald Farrer wrote an account of their natural habitat when he visited the Hpimaw Pass in Burma in the early twentieth century: 'Very cold in winter with snow, lying for a week at a time. Meanwhile in May comes the year's one burst of amiability and in June the rains break, and rain and rain in an almost uninterrupted succession of fog and gloom and deluges until October comes round with the fine clear weather of autumn and winter.' Some years this climatical observation is not too dissimilar to parts of Wales, so I will be persevering with the *Nomocharis* challenge.

The hardy waterside Japanese iris, *Iris ensata*, has been the subject of many years of selective breeding. The distinctive flowers are offset by sword-shaped foliage which provides architectural form. *Rogersia pinnata*, hostas and ferns are growing nearby.

Dominant shrubs in Bishop Rudd's Walk include various forms of hydrangea that add colour in late summer and early autumn. I don't mean the mopheads in bright pinks and blues but subtler, more distinguished types. Some of the finest specimens include *Hydrangea aspera* 'Anthony Bullivant', the many forms of *Hydrangea paniculata*, and *Hydrangea arborescens* 'Annabelle' and 'Bounty'. Another wonderful plant for autumn interest is also a member of the hydrangea family: *Kirengeshoma palmata*, an excellent herbaceous plant with large palmate leaves, which also produces attractive waxy yellow pendulous flowers.

Clerodendrum bungei is related to verbena. It is a suckering woody shrub introduced from China by the famous plant-hunter Robert Fortune. The soft pink fragrant flowers appear at the end of summer and are much admired. It was once considered to be tender, requiring a warm sheltered position, but this is not the case. I know of no other genera that have such pleasantly scented flowers – and such disgustingly foetid pungent leaves when bruised.

Because this area now contains some of the most beautiful plants in cultivation and a diversity seldom encountered in British gardens, if I had to choose my favourite part of the garden, it would be Bishop Rudd's Walk.

Left: *Kirengeshoma palmata* is a valuable late-flowering Japanese herbaceous plant. At the gentlest touch of frost it surrenders with dramatic suddenness.

Right, above and below: *Diphylleia cymosa* from the southern Appalachians is in the family Berberidaceae. Commonly known as umbrella leaf, it makes a good foliage plant; the short-lived flowers are followed in autumn by metallic blue fruits supported on red stems.

SEASONAL TREASURES

The labour of clearing the tangle of seedling trees and overgrown evergreens behind the mansion was offset by the excitement of combing the catalogues of specialist nurseries and compiling a wish-list of treasures to plant in what we decided to call Bishop Rudd's Walk. It was like Christmas each time the orders were delivered and the packages opened to reveal bulbs like the handful of *Fritillaria camschatcensis* (below). In the following pages I have gathered together a pictorial collection of some of the wonderful plants that can be found through the year in what has become my favourite part of the garden at Aberglasney.

NOMOCHARIS

Twenty years ago I recall seeing a plate illustrating *Nomocharis mairei* in Patrick M. Synge's book *Lilies*. (The genus is very closely related to true lilies.) I found it hard to believe that such a beautiful plant existed: the reason I had not encountered these cherished beauties is that their requirements are very specific, which limits their cultural range. For anyone who thinks meconopsis are temperamental, nomocharis are in a league of their own: they have an infuriating propensity not to reappear after flowering.

I was excited at the prospect of drifts of these Asiatic beauties, but alas it was not to be; the rare spells of dry weather during some summers were enough to weaken the plants' constitution and reduce their vigour. We grow – or endeavour to grow – *Nomocharis saluenensis* as well as *Nomocharis pardanthina*. Perseverance is necessary and we have chosen new damper surroundings in a bid to improve their cultural conditions.

Right: *Nomocharis pardanthina* must rate as one of the most exquisite bulbs that can be grown in temperate gardens.

SPRING STARS

Far left, above: *Glaucidium palmatum* var. *leucanthum* contrasts with a background of *Omphalodes cappadocica* 'Cherry Ingram'.

Far left, below: *Sanguinaria canadensis* f. *multiplex* is one of the most beautiful of all woodland plants, resembling a terrestrial water lily. It is a shame that the pure white flowers are so frustratingly fleeting, lasting little more than one day. The scalloped leaves that follow are distinctly attractive.

Near left: *Notholirion bulbiferum* is a native of China and seldom seen cultivated in gardens. Its tall flower spikes are very imposing and aristocratic in appearance. They have a habit of being monocarpic, but produce bulbils or seed for regeneration.

Right, above: *Hepatica transsilvanica* 'Blue Jewel' is a small, semi-evergreen perennial with violet-blue spring flowers. Treasured cultivars of the remarkably beautiful related species *Hepatica nobilis* can cost several hundred pounds each – not bad for a buttercup relative!

Right, below: Shortias are considered among the elite of garden plants. They are frustratingly slow to increase, and exorbitantly expensive. *Shortia uniflora* var. *orbicularis* 'Grandiflora' is an exquisite Japanese evergreen sub-shrub which grows in high woodland in Honshu. *Shortia soldanelloides* is another Japanese species, with flowers resembling those of soldanella.

Above: The dog's-tooth violet *Erythronium dens-canis* flowering through a moss-covered bank.

Near right: *Dodecatheon meadia* f. *album* is a member of the *Primula* family. It is commonly known as the American cowslip or shooting star, and is a welcome addition to a woodland border.

Centre: *Dicentra* 'Luxuriant' is a hybrid between two American species. The foliage is fern-like and light green in colour.

Far right: *Digitalis* 'Saltwood Summer' is a fascinating biennial foxglove discovered in Saltwood in Kent. It has white orchid-like flowers and four red-spotted curving petals. The lowest petal is particularly long, giving the flower a distinctive orchid-like appearance.

TRILLIUMS

Trilliums seem to do exceptionally well, naturalizing happily in the humus-rich soil in Bishop Rudd's Walk. They seem to have a particularly 'exotic' quality, perhaps because of their unfamiliarity and their very distinctive tripartite arrangement.

The highly desirable double-flowered Trillium grandiflorum 'Snowbunting' (above) is exquisitely beautiful, but is seldom seen in gardens. This form has to be propagated by asexual means, which is a very slow process, so plants command a very high price.

The white-flowered *Trillium grandiflorum* (right) is the most commonly grown trillium, but it still rates as one of the finest species for general cultivation in gardens. It is also one of the most beautiful. It is easy to cultivate and self-sown seedlings from the original plants are now growing and naturalizing nearby.

There is considerable variation in different trillium species, from the size and stature of the plant to the intricacies of the various flower forms. At Aberglasney I prefer to grow the different species in distinct groups, well away from one another so that each makes its own impact.

Far left, above: The lemon-scented, lemon-yellow flowers of *Trillium luteum* appear in early May and are accompanied by three distinctly mottled leaves. This species is sessile and lacks a flower stalk, but its attractive foliage makes a lovely foil around the bright flowers.

Far left, below: *Trillium undulatum* is known as the painted trillium because of the attractive markings on its undulating petals.

Left: *Trillium erectum* f. *albiflorum* has particularly curious flowers, with three green sepals and three white petals.

Right, above: *Trillium kurabayashii* is the first trillium to emerge and flower at Aberglasney, usually at the beginning of March. It is very easy to grow and has attractive mottled foliage with impressive large maroon petals to its sessile flowers. A recently discovered species native to the West Coast of the USA, it is named after the Japanese cytologist/geneticist who discovered it.

Right, below: The dwarf trillium, *Trillium pusillum* var. *pusillum*, is a charming diminutive species from the eastern USA, growing to only 5 cm in height. Careful cultivation is required to allow this little treasure to multiply naturally, by good initial soil preparation and ensuring there is no competition from more vigorous species.

PRIMULAS

Because they naturalize so readily in our damp soil, primulas add more colour to Bishop Rudd's Walk than any other genus. Indeed, some of the more colourful seedlings of the giant cowslip, *Primula florindae*, can combine to create a blend of bright pointillistic colour that from a distance looks like the dreaded orange so despised by tasteful gardeners. Most visitors, however, enjoy the cheerful display.

Right: The delightful small *Primula rosea* growing alongside the stream is the first of the primulas to flower.

Below left: *Primula alpicola* var. *violacea* is a magnificent form. Not only does it have beautiful heavily textured bi-coloured flowers, but these have an added bonus of being wonderfully fragrant, making it one of the most lovely of all garden primulas.

Below right: *Primula sieboldii* is a creeping rhizomatous Japanese primula which has been cultivated in Britain for many years.

Far right: *Primula florindae* is sometimes known as the giant cowslip and originates from southeastern Tibet. Its umbels are usually sulphur-yellow, but orange and red forms are also cultivated. It is a plant of stout constitution and is strongly fragrant.

Following pages, left: *Primula capitata* subsp. *mooreana* from Sikkim is valuable because it flowers in August and September, when woodland gardens are often devoid of much colour. This species has a farinose covering on the leaves, flower stem and flower. Right: A mass of naturalizing Asiatic primulas in early June, with meconopsis and foxgloves in the background.

ARISAEMAS

A genus that is becoming increasingly popular is *Arisaema*, plants grown as much for their beautiful architectural leaves as their unusual striped hooded spathes. Several species are grown in the garden, but the most majestic is the Asiatic *Arisaema speciosum*, which is one of the largest and most spectacular, growing to 1 metre in height.

It has huge architectural leaves (left), with attractively mottled markings on the leaf stem. The spathe (right) is dark maroon with white stripes, and has a remarkable tendril growing from the top that can reach a metre long. This conspicuous appendix acts as an access route to the spadex for pollinating insects.

Near right: *Arisaema consanguineum* has attractive palm-like leaves, which are highly ornamental. The elegant spathes are an added bonus. It also produces very unusual fruiting heads (above).

Centre right: A close-up image of the spadix of *Arisaema fargesii*, showing the remarkable striated markings of the spathe.

Far right: A species I particularly admire is *Arisaema candidissimum* from western China, possibly one of the best known and probably the most beautiful. It is a moderately small plant and its spathe, produced during June and July, is light pink with longitudinal white stripes.

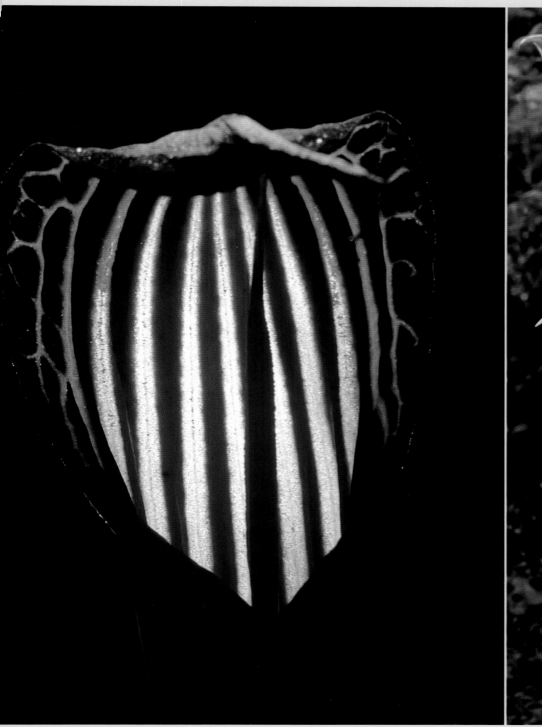

MECONOPSIS

The most exquisitely beautiful of all the herbaceous plants in Bishop Rudd's Walk must be the blue Himalayan poppy *Meconopsis grandis*, but unfortunately this short-lived perennial can just disappear without trace. It is completely intolerant of drought. In the right conditions it germinates easily (but rarely in situ), but can quickly damp off. When plants do thrive they require dividing every three years in order to perpetuate their magnificent display. Other species grown in this area include the charming yellow *Meconopsis villosa* and the blue and white forms of *Meconopsis betonicifolia*. I did grow the fickle bright red *Meconopsis punicea* a few years ago, but despite reports that some can be perennial, ours certainly were not. Because the pollen is not released at the same time as the stigma is receptive, saving seed is not straightforward, either. I take my hat off to those who persevere with this little jewel.

Right: A drift of *Meconopsis grandis* in Bishop Rudd's Walk, between the large leaves of *Astilboides tabularis* and the tall bright yellow *Primula helodoxa* (*prolifera*) in the foreground. The native foxglove makes a good companion.

Far right: The iridescent blue flowers of *Meconopsis grandis* with their contrasting golden anthers are universally admired, but these plants can be temperamental.

Following pages, left: *Meconopsis betonicifolia* var. *alba* is perennial, but usually behaves more like a biennial. It is thought that removing the first flower buds helps to ensure perennation, but it is a hard-hearted gardener who has the willpower to do so.

Right: *Meconopsis villosa* (previously called *Cathcartia villosa*) is a Himalayan woodland species. It is a stunningly beautiful poppy, having the purest radiant yellow flowers combined with hairy palmately lobed leaves. Like most *Meconopsis*, it is not reliably perennial and should be raised from seed regularly to ensure its continued cultivation.

AUTUMN STARS

Spring comes in with such a fanfare, and is particularly welcome after the barrenness of winter, so it is pleasing to find a number of plants that save their performance until later in the season.

Left: The excellent *Saxifraga cortusifolia* 'Ruby Wedding' would be worth having for its sumptuous ruby-red variegated leaves, but the orchid-like dainty pink flowers put it into a class of its own. If only it was easier to grow!

Opposite, top left: The autumnal foliage of *Galax urceolata* is probably the most ornamental attribute of this creeping evergreen perennial from the northeastern USA.

Opposite, top right: The fragrant late-summer flowers of *Clerodendrum bungei*, a shrub related to verbena.

Opposite, bottom left: The genus *Tricyrtis* was once in the lily family, but is now placed in the lily-of-the-valley family Convallariaceae. *Tricyrtis* 'White Towers' is a cultivar with attractive hairy foliage and develops spotted orchid-like upward-facing flowers – commonly known as toad lilies – during late autumn.

Opposite, bottom right: *Rhododendron luteum* is a well-known azalea, which is sometimes used as a rootstock for grafting. The yellow flowers are highly fragrant. The plants growing at Aberglasney were raised from seed collected from good autumn-colouring forms.

Following pages: *Actaea matsumurae* 'White Pearl', in detail (left) and in context as a graceful, willowy plant with wand-like flower stems (right). Formerly known as Cimicifuga, this flowers during the autumn, making a valuable contribution to Bishop Rudd's Walk, with the bonus of being fragrant. Although showing no resemblance to the buttercup, it is in the family Ranunculaceae.

Left: Like many *Hydrangea paniculata* cultivars, 'Grandiflora' offers months of flowering from late summer through to autumn. The fertile flowers themselves are very small and insignificant; the impact is made by the large infertile flowers, which attract the notice of pollinating insects. The plants are best pruned annually to achieve larger panicles and to maintain a compact habit.

Right: *Hydrangea arborescens* 'Annabelle' is a superb plant for a damp area. The long-lasting plumes of flower are much appreciated towards the end of summer, when little else makes such a magnificent display.

Following pages: *Ilex* x *attenuata* 'Sunny Foster' (left) was discovered in the US National Arboretum in 1964 and first released to the trade in 1982. It comes into its own during the winter months, when the bright yellow foliage glows in the sun. *Enkianthus campanulatus*, a Japanese member of the Ericaceae, is a slow-growing plant with fiery autumn foliage, seen (far right) alongside the path on the northern side of Bishop Rudd's Walk. Its cultivar *Enkianthus campanulatus* 'Red Bells' (centre) has beautiful lantern-like heather flowers with distinctive red margins

THE ASIATIC GARDEN

This area has been created since 2004. It is not part of the original garden complex, but to make it we have colonized a stretch of what used to be called Cae Ceffyl – horse field – next to the upper part of Bishop Rudd's Walk. In fact this is the highest point in the garden. The raised mound with the oriental-looking seat was erected in 2005 to give views down the Tywi valley with the flank of Grongaer Hill on one side and Merlin's Hill on the other, giving a view of Carmarthen in the distance. After the steep pull uphill to this point, many visitors are all too ready to pause here and rest, admiring the view as well as contemplating the plants they have just seen, and planning what to look at on the way back down on the other side of the ravine.

All the plants originate from various parts of Asia, including China, Japan, Korea, Tibet and Nepal – prime sources for plant-hunters of the last few centuries, and even today, since plants from those regions adapt very well to our British climate. As in the rest of the garden the planting has been chosen to be of interest throughout the year, not just for flowers, but also for interesting bark, foliage and perfume.

During January and February the collection of witch hazels has a range of

Left: *Acer palmatum* 'Trompenburg' is a fine maple with exceptional autumn colour. It was named after the renowned arboretum in Rotterdam.

Right: The oriental structure resembling a Japanese Torii Gate is situated at the top of the Asiatic garden with a collection of Japanese azaleas lining the path. The red *Azalea* 'Santa Maria' is in the foreground.

coloured flowers, including yellow, red and orange. All have a fragrance, but the yellow forms are usually the most wonderfully scented. The subtle, strange, strap-like twisted petals on bare stems merit close scrutiny. I think the flowers of hamamelis are one of nature's miracles, because despite long periods of freezing weather, the delicate-looking petals are not even blemished.

Hamamelis x *intermedia* 'Pallida' is often quoted as one of the best varieties to plant; it does flower well, but the fragrance of the flower is not the sweetest. An even less desirable attribute is that it sometimes (particularly on younger specimens) retains the dead brown leaves of the previous year, which I find particularly unappealing. I resort to pulling them off by hand.

During the winter various unusual conifers stand out, including an umbrella pine, *Sciadopitys verticillata* 'Green Globe', and a lace-bark pine, *Pinus bungeana*, which was first discovered in 1831 in a temple garden in Peking by Dr Bunge and introduced by the Scottish botanist and plant-hunter Robert Fortune in 1846. When mature it has one of the most strikingly attractive bark patterns of any tree, resembling that of a London plane, with exfoliating flakes. The most beautiful specimen I have seen is a multi-stemmed tree that grows at the United States National Arboretum in Washington DC, near the azalea collection. It is very slow-growing, rarely exceeding 15 cm a year. There are lots of attractive pines, but personally I think this one is the loveliest of all.

I am always apprehensive about the wellbeing of two trees in the Magnoliaceae during the winter months. They have recently been reclassified from the genera *Michelia* and *Manglietia* to *Magnolia* itself. *Magnolia doltsopa* grows in the Upper Walled Garden, but *Magnolia insignis* (formerly *Manglietia*

insignis*) is planted here, in a more exposed position. This species is decidedly tender and always looks rather scruffy by the end of the winter. I should really give up on it and dig it out, but as it was given to me by a friend who grew it from seed he collected in China, I shall continue to persevere for a few more years.

Spring is the most colourful season when many of the rhododendrons, azaleas and camellias flower, and the cherry and magnolia blossoms are at their most magnificent. During late spring and early summer there is a large collection of both tree and herbaceous peonies, some of which were grown from seed collected from a fine form of *Paeonia suffruticosa* with attractive leaves and stunning large purple papery flowers.

These are followed by a collection of Asiatic lilies and the beautiful but unfortunately named toad lily (*Tricyrtis*), which are wonderful autumn-flowering herbaceous plants for dappled shade. The flowers are

Opposite: *Prunus mume* 'Beni-chidori' is known as the Japanese apricot. It is a small tree and flowers in late February and March. The modest individual flowers are remarkably beautiful, with crimson-pink petals and an addictively sweet perfume (see pages 166–7).

Above: *Camellia* 'Cinnamon Cindy' is a delightful upright-growing camellia, raised in New Zealand, which has become available in the UK in the past 10 years.

Following pages, left: *Tricyrtis hirta* is an interesting Japanese perennial valuable for its autumn flowering. The individual 'toad lily' flowers are peculiar in their appearance, but remarkably beautiful.

Right: *Lilium* 'Black Beauty' is a robust and beautiful lily; although the long-lasting flowers resemble those of *Lilium speciosum*, it lacks their heavy fragrance.

usually white marked with purple, but yellow, pink and white forms are also available.

The collection of maples is particularly striking in the spring and autumn and includes many unusual species such as *Acer campbellii* subsp. *flabellatum* var. *yunnanense* and a handsome specimen of the finely leafed *Acer palmatum* 'Red Filigree Lace', which is considered to be one of the most beautiful and unusual maple introductions. It originated as a chance seedling in a garden in Oregon. The specimen at Aberglasney is one of the largest in the country. It is a grafted plant imported from New Zealand in 1989 and had been grown in a large container until it was planted out in 2004. It has since been joined by several other choice Japanese maple varieties.

Previous pages: *Cornus* 'Porlock' (left) is one of a pair of beautiful dogwood hybrids that were discovered in a garden in Somerset. Their assumed parents are the deciduous *Cornus kousa* and the evergreen *Cornus capitata*.

Paeonia 'Black Pirate' (right) has dramatic, deep mahogany-red semi-double flowers and finely dissected foliage. It is one of the most exquisite tree peonies available, and correspondingly one of the most expensive to purchase.

This page: left, above: *Camellia* x *vernalis* 'Yuletide' is another excellent recent introduction from Nuccio's Nurseries in California. It starts to flower over the Christmas period.

Left, below: *Magnolia* x *loebneri* 'Donna' is a vigorous plant that produces large white flat flowers with broad petals.

Right: The Asiatic Garden with its fine collection of Japanese maples and dwarf rhododendrons already creating a colourful display in early spring.

Previous pages: *Meconopsis napaulensis* is one of the most gorgeous herbaceous plants that can be grown. The stunning silver evergreen rosettes make this species one of the most attractive foliage plants in the Asiatic Garden. During the summer the leaves are complimented by a range of different coloured flowers, including this sumptuous red. Unfortunately this species is monocarpic, so after flowering the plant will die, but it can be perpetuated by sowing seed.

This page: Early spring foliage of *Meconopsis napaulensis*, peonies and maples with early-flowering camellias and dwarf rhododendrons.

Following pages, left: *Acer griseum*, known as the paperbark maple, is a stunningly beautiful tree. It was originally introduced from China in 1901 by Ernest Wilson. This particular tree was grown from selected seed collected in 1992.

Right: *Malus* x *robusta* 'Red Sentinel' has persistent fruits that last long into the winter.

While Bishop Rudd's Walk together with the Asiatic Garden can be found by heading uphill from the house, essentially following the stream, there is a more amorphous area of garden on the lower slope. It occupies an area of ground above the Upper Walled Garden, roughly between the south façade of the mansion and the fence marking the boundary with the fields of Berllan Dywyll Farm. As with the gardens up the hill, the areas such as the Rose Border and Alpinum blend into one another with no distinct dividing line, making it impossible to describe a definitive route.

The lower hillside area can be approached from Bishop Rudd's Walk, but can also be accessed from the southwest corner of the house or by a pathway that leads from the door in the southern wall of the Upper Walled Garden. The east wall at the top of the Upper Walled Garden is a retaining wall, creating a terrace. The old path running along the top of this wall provides an opportunity to gaze down on Penelope Hobhouse's layout with its concentric ellipses and also leads you past the Aviaries, a controversial historic feature – which I'll come to in due course – but from the proximity of the house you might be tempted to fork off uphill instead, especially if the roses are in bloom.

We created the Rose Border in 2004 by dissecting one of the larger planting areas near the house into two by introducing a narrow path. I find it quite frustrating when I

A misty morning with *Primula florindae*, the dark maroon foliage of *Ligularia dentata* 'Desdemona' and the rambling rose 'Paul's Himalayan Musk'

come across a large border in a garden where an absence of paths prevents you from getting close to the plants within it – especially fragrant ones, making them inaccessible to the nose.

Annual dressing with organic matter has a beneficial effect, but the only opportunity to create a really good fertile border is by good preparation before it is planted. Several tonnes of well-rotted horse manure was dug deep into the ground here, as well as being mixed in with the topsoil.

The Rose Border contains a collection of fragrant old-fashioned roses underplanted with companion plants such as tiarella, geraniums, heuchera, brunnera and nepeta. The roses are at their peak in June and July, when they are much admired, but they continue flowering sporadically through to the autumn.

There are also some larger shrubs which act as a backdrop. Magnolias, corylopsis and viburnums add interest during the spring before the roses flower and a *Eucryphia* x *nymansensis* flowers towards the end of the summer with its pure white flowers and conspicuous stamens.

It has to be said that the high rainfall of this part of the country is not best suited for rose growing, as fungal problems are prone to develop. It is necessary to select cultivars which are less susceptible to mildew and blackspot. The roses are mulched annually

Left: An autumn view from the path above the Rose Border looking across the garden's ancient crenellated walls.

Right: *Magnolia stellata* 'Jane Platt' grows near the northern side of the Aviaries. It is the best pink form available; its only fault is that unlike the species it has no fragrance.

with manure, which not only has the benefit of keeping the soil fertile and helping keep the roses healthy, but also helps control the blackspot by smothering latent spores at the base of the roses.

THE AVIARIES

The set of six Victorian caged enclosures was originally built in the 1870s for rearing ornamental pheasants. When the Aberglasney Restoration Trust purchased the property, the decrepit aviaries were hardly visible in the covering of undergrowth. With the vegetation removed, the structure was in such a poor condition that restoration seemed almost futile. In search of inspiration, I visited the famous aviaries at Waddesdon Manor in Buckinghamshire, but I was in for a shock. The Waddesdon aviaries built for Baron Ferdinand de Rothschild are made of cast iron in the style of a rococo trelliswork pavilion, such as those erected at Versailles, complete with copious amounts of gold leaf for decoration. Our aviaries were built of serviceable yellow brick: there could not have been a more stark contrast. On my return

Left: The Rose Border contains a collection of old-fashioned roses with mixed herbaceous underplanting. The roses are at their peak in June and July, when their fragrance is much admired.

Right: The vigorous rose 'Rosemary Foster', which originated at Maurice and Rosemary Foster's garden in Ivy Hatch, Kent. In the foreground is *Persicaria affinis* 'Superba', an amazing impenetrable ground-covering plant that flowers for at least four months of the year.

there seemed to be only one sensible solution and that was to remove them altogether, but being a listed structure, they couldn't simply be demolished.

As the area surrounding the aviaries became cultivated, the dilapidated state of the tumbledown buildings became even more of an eyesore. This was remarked upon one day by a couple who visited Aberglasney regularly. When the situation was explained to them, they very generously offered to donate the majority of the funding needed for restoration. This commenced in 2006; due to the buildings' instability, the majority of the structure that remained standing had to be carefully dismantled and rebuilt.

Once restored, much debate took place about the future use of this now prominent feature. We were particularly concerned about the ethical and financial implications of the buildings' original use – to house a collection of ornamental pheasants. The eventual decision was not to keep birds in captivity but to find an alternative use.

The solution was rather paradoxical. As much as I enjoy the presence of birds in the garden, I became distraught a few years ago when I noticed that a pair of bullfinches had stripped every one of the buds from one of my favourite trees in the garden – *Prunus mume* 'Beni-Chidori', the Japanese apricot.

Left: Flowers of the exuberant rose 'Bobbie James' mingle with those of *Philadelphus* 'Belle Etoile', a delightfully fragrant variety which received a Royal Horticultural Society award as early as 1930. The pink rose in the foreground is 'Gertrude Jekyll'.

Right: *Rosa moyesii* 'Geranium'. This cultivar was raised at Wisley Gardens. The bright red flowers are followed by beautiful hips in the autumn

THE AVIARIES

The fate of the Aviaries, which occupy a key position on the terrace overlooking the Upper Walled Garden, parallels that of Aberglasney – from dereliction to re-creation. The fact that they were listed buildings meant that they had to be retained, but we engineered a role reversal, and now keep birds *out* rather than *in*.

Somewhere in the tangle of vegetation (left, above) it is possible to detect the curving metal frames of some dilapidated structures. One wall remained standing (left, below) – with support – after the site was cleared for restoration. The newly restored Aviaries in 2006 (far right, above), before plants were introduced.

The Aviaries also serve as signposts. Uphill from the Aviaries, the lovely *Magnolia* x *loebneri* 'Merrill' (far right, below), raised in 1939 at the Arnold Arboretum. In the foreground is *Corylopsis spicata* with a wonderful display of delightful primrose-yellow flowers on bare twigs in April.

Centre: The flower of *Prunus mume* 'Beni-chidori' – its ravishing by bullfinches prompted my solution to the question of how to plant the restored Aviaries.

Although bullfinches are beautiful birds, they have had a long reputation for being troublesome. As early as 1566 an Act of Parliament put a penny bounty on the head of 'everie bullfynche'.

I don't consider myself particularly vindictive, but the aviaries provided a ready-made opportunity to turn the tables. I decided to grow different strawberries in each cage, and to train dwarf cherries on the walls. We now use the cage structures to keep wild birds *out* rather than keep tame birds *in*. Every time I see frustrated birds hopping around the cage trying to get at the ripening fruit, I think of that poor denuded *Prunus mume*, and don't feel so bad.

Having solved the bird problem, the smile was soon wiped off my face once again: it became apparent that it wasn't nature's intention to make it easy for me. Field mice soon noticed the seasonal bounty and made it blatantly obvious that the gastronomic feast of ripe strawberries was for sharing. I wouldn't have minded so much if they gorged on them, but to have them merely sample every single one seems decidedly spiteful.

Left: This *Hamamelis* x *intermedia* was purchased as the cultivar 'Nina', but research has proved that several forms were erroneously distributed by a nurseryman under that name; therefore 'Nina' is incorrect and the true name of this witch hazel unknown.

Right: The lovely combination of *Magnolia stellata* 'Centennial' with *Narcissus* 'Trena' and *Narcissus* 'Lemon Silk' outside the Upper Walled Garden, beside the path leading up towards the aviary terrace and the Alpinum.

THE ALPINUM

This feature was constructed in 2007 to allow us to cultivate diminutive plants such as alpines and small woody shrubs. The term 'Alpinum' was taken from a similar feature in the late eighteenth-century landscape garden created by Thomas Johnes at Hafod near Aberystwyth, which was once one of the finest picturesque estates in Britain. Our Alpinum took the place of a rather nondescript small pond, fed by a small spring which used to dry up in the summer months, making the water stagnant. The spring is now piped underground and the area has been cleared of inferior trees and vegetation, creating an open, west-facing site where our boundary makes a dog-leg angle towards the fields of neighbouring Berllan Dywyll farm.

The large blocks of limestone were selected from a local quarry and are typical of the stone used in the locality for building. The stone is of palaeontological interest as it contains numerous fossil invertebrates, so you occasionally see curious visitors scrutinizing the stones as well as, or instead of, the plants. It may look as if the rocks all fitted naturally into place: if only they had been that accommodating! Almost without exception, each rock had to be shaped to fit. This was no easy task, as the rock and the hammer seemed to possess the same density. Without the benefit of large earthmoving machinery, just positioning four rocks a day was considered highly productive and extremely exhausting. It certainly made me

The best gardens offer occasional views outwards as well as within. A winter view from the seat at the top of the Alpinum looks across the Tywi valley to the hills beyond.

Above: Initial clearance of the future Alpinum site took place during the winter of 2001 by felling the seedling ash trees and removing all the tree stumps.

Right: A spring view looking up the Alpinum, with a stunning (but as yet unnamed) magnolia. *Narcissus* 'Swallow', a charming recently introduced dwarf *cyclamineus* cultivar, is in the foreground.

appreciate what a daunting feat it must have been to move the Bluestone from the nearby Preseli Mountains to Stonehenge. It is our intention to extend the existing terracing sometime in the future, when time and energy permit, thus making this feature even more interesting.

Once the rocks were in position, a fine grit was added to the soil to help the drainage that many of the smaller plants would benefit

from. Several mature plants of an appropriate scale were dug up from other parts of the garden and replanted in this area, which added some instant maturity and gave the individual specimens prominence. They, like many of the mature plants around the garden, are a constant remainder of places I have visited and the generosity of fellow plant enthusiasts.

One very rare plant in the Alpinum is the Japanese holly *Ilex crenata* 'Dwarf Pagoda', raised from a cutting I was given twenty years ago. Another rarity, the very slender fastigiate yew *Taxus baccata* 'Green Column', was purchased in 1987 from a conifer specialist during a plant-buying trip in Holland. Both of these are slow-growing, a factor that partly accounts for their rarity.

Other notable plants include a mature specimen of the prostrate *Rhododendron serpyllifolium*, again from a cutting given to me in 1993. It is known as the wild thyme azalea, and has the smallest leaves of any rhododendron, measuring only 4 mm in length. The flowers are pale pink and only a centimetre across. Although it is not the most alluring of plants even when it is in full flower, it is worthy of cultivation, if only to illustrate the huge diversity of the genus.

The tiered raised beds and the sunken path between them enable smaller plants to be admired at a closer range. This is particularly appropriate for plants with intricate small flowers and for plants that have a delightful fragrance. For this reason, a number of dwarf daphnes and dianthus are grown, and their sweet perfume can be appreciated at close quarters.

Some of the flowers merit much closer inspection to appreciate them fully – the patterns on auriculated primulas, the amazing blue gentians with their striated

markings running down the throat of the flower, and the intricately frilled petals of soldanellas, to name but a few. It is often the case that the smaller the plant the more fascinating they become, not just the flowers, but the intricacy and diverse textural variations of the leaves. My close-up photographs often reveal details that are barely perceptible to the eye. Little delights me more than to spot a visitor peering into the heart of a flower and to relish its intricacies. When I see this I recognize a kindred spirit.

Left: *Cornus sanguinea* 'Midwinter Fire' was discovered in a garden in Germany around 1980 and was bought by a Dutch nursery and named in 1990. It is a brilliant plant for brightening up the garden during the bleak winter months, but make sure it is planted where the winter sun can set it alight.

Above: This tiny little buttercup, *Ranunculus alpestris*, is native to the European Alps. The pure white flowers are no more than 2 cm across and glisten in the late evening spring light.

ALPINE TREASURES

Far left, above: *Daphne jezoensis* was first introduced to Britain in the early 1960s from northern Honshu in Japan. It produces scented flowers during the late winter and early spring. There is variation within the species from the depth of flower colour to the perceptible scent.

Far left, below: I much prefer the smaller tulip species to the larger hybrid cultivars. *Tulipa bakeri* 'Lilac Wonder' blooms as early as the end of March. Baker's tulip is a common wildflower on the island of Crete, and this selected form, 'Lilac Wonder', was introduced in 1971.

Centre left, above: *Soldanella alpina* 'Alba' is a rare white form of the alpine snowbell.

Centre left, below: *Ranunculus calandrinioides* is an aristocratic buttercup from the Atlas Mountains in Morocco. It is usually recommended for the protection of an alpine house, but survived the severe cold temperatures of early 2009 at Aberglasney.

Near left: *Pulsatilla vernalis* comes from the European Alps and is acclaimed by some as the most lovely of all alpine flowers.

Above: *Ilex crenata* 'Dwarf Pagoda' is a very rare slow-growing holly. This female clone was developed at the National Arboretum in Washington, DC, and is not generally available in the UK.

Centre, above: *Daphne cneorum* 'Benaco' is a beautiful form of the garland flower with slightly narrower leaves than usual and a wonderful heady perfume.

Centre, below: *Daphne* x *susannae* 'Anton Fahndrich' is a hybrid between *Daphne arbuscula* and *Daphne collina*. The fragrant bright pink flowers appear in April–May.

Far right: *Muscari armeniacum* 'Cantab' braving the winter weather.

CHAPTER FIVE

THE POOL
AND BEYOND

It is now time to move into a series of diverse garden areas to the west of the historic walled gardens, where the sense of focus on the mansion is less evident, and away from the predominance of those high walls. Looking west from the Parapet Walk, you get a sense of openness as the ground falls away – and of the countryside, with Grongaer Hill rising as its backdrop. This is the landscape that John Dyer loved and wrote about.

The Pool Garden is actually a transitional space, dominated by the high outer wall of the Parapet Walk, and also bounded to the north by a high wall. To the south and west, however, the enclosing walls are low ones. This is also a historical space. A pool must have been here since earliest times, although the rectangular shape is probably Victorian.

The other westerly 'gardens' are part of the heritage of the larger estate of former times, when the property amounted to well over a thousand acres, with tenant farms as well as the Home Farm. The woodland would have been a source of timber and would have provided cover for game.

Previous pages: The simple landscaping of smooth mown grass immediately around the pool maintains the calm atmosphere.

Left: Native trees and perennials predominate in Pigeon House Wood, to the southwest of the Pool Garden, enhanced by exotics that enjoy the shade and moisture.

Right: A winter view looking across the pool from the Cloister Garden archway to the weeping ash on the opposite west bank – a venerable tree that is majestic in all lights and at all seasons (see following pages).

THE POOL GARDEN

It is thought that the pool has medieval origins; it has certainly changed shape during its long history. It collects the water from several springs, including one which originates underneath the mansion's cellar. Another major source is a stream which starts from a spring near the church in the village. It runs down the valley through Bishop Rudd's Walk and eventually flows over the high wall on the eastern side of the mansion before being piped underground to the pool. I suspect that water has followed the same course for hundreds of years.

When the Trust began work, the pool had been neglected for many years. It had silted up and lost its water-retentive lining, and seedling trees had sprouted where there should have been water. The walls have subsequently been rebuilt and the pool relined with clay.

The feature adds life to the garden in more ways than one. It is now home to a host of varied wildlife including eels, fish, newts,

Above: An improbable scene from the 1960s, when cattle were allowed to graze around and in the waterless pool. Only the parapet wall and the glimpse of the house in the background confirm the location of this pastoral scene.

Right: A new greenhouse was built on the footprint of an original Victorian structure in 2002 and is now used to house the citrus fruit during the winter.

frogs and toads, which moved in voluntarily after the restoration. Soon after Aberglasney's opening, a kind local lady offered her collection of valuable koi carp, which were gratefully received. However, this gourmet food was too tempting for the discriminating local otter, which made its way upstream from the main river in the valley. It is still a regular visitor, but now feeds on the copious number of eels. Among the most wonderful sights at Aberglasney are the acrobatic birds, which feed on the insects over the pool. They include swallows, house martins, sand martins and occasional swifts. And for those fortunate enough to be near the pool at dusk, there is a repeat performance by the long-lived Daubenton's bats, which skim the surface with incredible precision; their alternative name is water bat. A reward for starting work early is to see the elusive kingfisher that visits regularly throughout the year.

The Pool Garden lies to the west of the Cloister Garden and can be viewed from the Parapet Walk, which makes an ideal viewing point to gaze down on the expanse of water. The battered outer wall of the Cloister range looks particularly high from the western approach, because the ground slopes away, down to the smooth grassy bank edging the pool. The archives contain a photograph

A long rectangular bed on the site of the old Victorian vinery provides the Pool Garden with its single splash of colourful floral decoration. A framework of dwarf box is the basis for seasonal bedding, which varies slightly from year to year. Tulips are a spring essential: the dark 'Queen of Night' (left), is late flowering, and contrasts well with pale yellow wallflowers. Another year the elegant *Tulipa* 'Burgundy' (right) is chosen to make a spectacular display.

taken about a century ago showing three gardeners standing here beside some box-edged planting beds – just the sort of floral embellishment that the Victorians and Edwardians loved to create, and that we are happy to forget. It is the simplicity of the landscape that makes this area so restful – an expanse of grass with no augmentation. The planting policy around the pond is also deliberately minimalist so as not to upstage the water feature.

One surviving tree is particularly majestic: the venerable weeping ash on the western boundary of the Pool Garden, whose reflection in the still pool surface mirrors its drooping, curving branches. The ash is my least favourite of all our British native trees. They are gross feeders, brittle and one of the last to come into leaf; the black flowers are insignificant, the leaves fall quickly, they have little autumn colour and their ability to self-seed in this part of the country is only equalled by the sycamore. Its main commercial use is for tool handles; personally I have pleasure using it for firewood.

The weeping ash *Fraxinus excelsior* 'Pendula', however, is in a different class. It has been cultivated since the early eighteenth century. As is the case with the Aberglasney tree, there is usually a visible graft union somewhere on the main trunk. Apparently a specimen at Elvaston Castle in Derbyshire was grafted 27 metres up the trunk of a common ash. The silhouette of the tree at Aberglasney is recognizable in a photograph taken in around 1870, which would make it at the very least 150 years of age.

The one patch of purely ornamental planting in this garden area is in a long rectangle against the north wall. It marks the site of what must once have been Aberglasney's Victorian pride and joy: a vinery. Archaeologists uncovered the row of red-brick vine arches, which allowed the roots of the vine to access the fertile soil outside the vinery, while the fruiting stems were trained inside under the protection of the glass. Like the two walled gardens, this site serves as a reminder of the fact that in days gone by they 'grew their own' – a testament to the skills of past gardeners, who by endless ingenuity were able to provide for the 'big house' all year round. Here, in a diaper pattern of dwarf box, we now ring the changes with seasonal planting of tulips and wallflowers in spring and marguerites or salvias in the summer.

The area abuts the paved terrace near the café. The south- and west-facing walls here act as a sun-trap and call for sun-loving woody plants. The terrace has been the home of what must be the least significant-looking plant in the garden: *Aloysia triphylla*, previously known as *Lippia citriodora*, the lemon verbena. It is native of Argentina and Chile and the leaves are pungently lemon-scented – I can smell it just thinking about it. The poor plant gets denuded as I pinch off leaves and growing tips to hand to groups of unsuspecting visitors to enjoy.

In the corner is one of my favourite climbers, the star jasmine *Trachelospermum jasminoides*, which has already reached the eaves of the roof. It is an Asiatic plant with evergreen leaves that turn scarlet during the winter. The flowers are produced from mid to late summer and are heavily perfumed. It was introduced by Robert Fortune in 1844.

Magnolia grandiflora is probably the most distinctive ornamental evergreen for a south- or west-facing wall. The fruity lemon-scented flowers appear sporadically during mid to late summer. Unfortunately, I inherited this plant when I arrived. Why unfortunately? Because there are over a

hundred different cultivars of this handsome plant, from miniatures to giants. A slower-growing form would have been more desirable on the confined outer walls of the building.

The other handsome plant with large evergreen leaves is the loquat, *Eriobotrya japonica*. Apart from the attractive leaves, the flowers that appear intermittently during the winter and early spring have a strong fragrance. The flowers resemble those of hawthorn, and like hawthorn it is a member of the rose family. It fruited for the first time in 2008. Maybe it was just the ones I tried, but they didn't taste as nice as they looked.

Above: Planted in the Meadow near the wall of the Pool Garden is the stunning new *Magnolia* 'Felix Jury'. Raised in New Zealand by Mark Jury, its magnificent colour is derived from having *M. campbellii* subsp. *mollicomata* 'Lanarth' in its parentage.

Opposite: The luxuriant winter foliage of *Trachelospermum jasminoides* clothing the west-facing wall of the café, formerly the gardener's cottage.

THE MEADOW

This grassy open space lies just downhill from the Pool Garden. It dips into a shallow valley to accommodate the outfall from the pool as it turns into the stream running away towards Pigeon House Wood. With its apparently natural, uncultivated atmosphere, it makes a contrast to the formal garden spaces, especially the adjacent Lower Walled Garden with its busy rows of vegetables and flowers.

The meadow is such a seemingly undemanding area that visitors often just walk through on the way to explore Pigeon House Wood. Others, in contrast, pause here to view the expanse of pastoral landscape. Outside the ever-present walls of the main complex of gardens, there is a sense of greenness. It continues almost seamlessly beyond the boundary into the soft rolling fields that lead down to the Tywi valley – just the countryside that John Dyer knew and celebrated in his poetry. It is a reminder of where we are, a garden in the landscape.

Of course none of this is 'natural'. Even the fields are managed and cultivated in some way. This is even more true of apparently 'natural' garden areas, a fact that is quite evident to people who come here in the spring. We have planted the meadow with a mixture of several thousand *Narcissus bulbocodium*, also known as the hoop-petticoat daffodil, which is native to the Iberian Peninsula and northwestern Africa, and *Fritillaria meleagris*, the snake's-head

Looking south through the deer fence down to the misty Tywi valley with the beautiful tessellated flowers of *Fritillaria meleagris* and the dainty *Narcissus bulbocodium* in the foreground.

fritillary – a European species occasionally found growing wild in the UK. It is hoped that in years to come the damp meadow will be carpeted by the seeding bulbs. To encourage this, the meadow is not cut until the seeds have dispersed, usually not before the end of July. The grass is then mown regularly during drier weather, to keep the sward short in preparation for the bulbs to appear the following year.

To compliment the natural look and to add seasonal interest, we have planted a small collection of six different crab apples in the meadow. They are highly ornamental garden trees, which are attractive in flower and fruit – which can be red, orange, pink or yellow – and some also have good autumn colour. *Malus* x *atrosanguinea* 'Gorgeous' is one of my favourites, and lives up to its name. It has pale pink flowers in April and intensely glossy, relatively large deep red fruit, which look like a miniature version of the American 'Empire' apple; they look good enough to eat raw – but don't be deceived.

Despite being introduced from Japan as long ago as 1862, *Malus floribunda* is still one of the most beautiful crab apples and holds its own for floral beauty. The dark crimson buds open to a pale pink, then fade to blush-white, but come out in succession giving a colourful contrast.

Left: A selection of crab apples flowering in the Meadow, with a glimpse of the greenhouse and vinery border in the background.

Right: Sedge beside the stream during the middle of winter.

PIGEON HOUSE WOOD

This historical name implies that there was once a pigeon house somewhere nearby, but to date no evidence of the structure has been found. There is a cottage halfway up Grongaer Hill named Pigeon House Cottage, now in private ownership, which is where Bishop Rudd's stone-built bathhouse is situated; a long way to go for a bath, but certainly out of the way of inquisitive eyes.

There are no walls here, and the formality of the main garden complex merges into a wooded glade, sculpted by streams which flow on down the valley into the meandering Tywi river. Ancient oaks line the boundary, but it is the handsome towering beech which dominate the upper area. Beech woodlands are scarce in this part of Wales. Beech is not native to the area, preferring the drier soils of the eastern counties, indicating that the trees here are a plantation crop of the nineteenth century. One might think that dappled shade, flowing streams and a humus-rich soil would be utopia for a gardener, but beech is a hungry, shallow-rooting tree, making the ground inhospitable for many desirable plants. The one woodland species that thrives

Above: The early purple orchid *Orchis mascula* in flower in Pigeon House Wood.

Right: The woodland floor carpeted with bluebells, with the emerging leaves of *Gunnera manicata* in the foreground.

in such conditions is the native bluebell, which blankets the ground in spring before the beech canopy closes over.

The woodland floor on the way to the beech plantation erupts with other native flora, which include wood anemones, primroses and wild garlic, making this one of the most beautiful areas of the whole garden. The wood also contains two native wild orchids, the early purple orchid (*Orchis mascula*) and the less easily noticeable broad-leaved helleborine (*Epipactis helleborine*), both of which I suspect to have been there for hundreds of years. The native epiphytic common polypody fern *Polypodium vulgare* is particularly noticeable growing on the older trees and is an indication of the high rainfall of the local area.

The sympathetic planting of some non-native species has augmented the habitat; these include varieties of dog's-tooth violet (*Erythronium*) and the double form of the Canadian bloodroot (*Sanguinaria canadensis* f. *multiplex* 'Plena'), which is quite at home and slowly increasing.

Previous pages: The native woodland flora is charming in its own right, but the introduced dog's-tooth violet *Erythronium* 'Pagoda' naturalizes equally happily with wood anemones *Anemone nemorosa* (left) and bluebells (right).

Left: Spathes of *Lysichiton americanus*, commonly known as the American skunk cabbage, emerging in the spring in the damp soil along the stream.

Right: As with the herbaceous plants, the native trees in Pigeon House Wood have been augmented by exotic shrubs like rhododendrons, which flourish in the understorey. The *Rhododendron sinogrande* in the foreground was grown from seed sown in 1998.

The American skunk cabbage (*Lysichiton americanus*) has been planted along the stream edge and in spring its bright yellow spathes punctuate the valley floor – giving the air a distinctive odour – before the waist-high light green leaves emerge and blend into the greens of summer shade.

Darmera peltata (previously known as *Peltiphyllum peltatum*) is another American introduction that adds interest to the boggy areas, firstly with its tall, leafless flower stems domed with heads of pale pink flowers that appear in late spring, which are then followed by attractive large leaves at the start of summer.

The giant rhubarb (*Gunnera manicata*) is named after the eighteenth-century Norwegian bishop and botanist, Ernst Gunnerus. It is native of swampy areas of southern Brazil and Colombia and must rate as the most dramatic foliage plant that can be grown in the British Isles. I derive much enjoyment when I see children walking underneath the huge natural umbrellas in total amazement; it is worth growing just for that. When you see the extreme lengths that people who have less favourable climates than ours will go to cultivate it, I realize how fortunate we are to be in a mild temperate area. Protecting the dormant crowns during the winter is not usually necessary here – but nature often has a nasty habit of punishing gardeners who become complacent about such things.

To augment the native trees a few exotics have also been introduced. The most notable is the large-leaved *Magnolia macrophylla*, which has the largest deciduous leaves of any tree that can be grown in this country, measuring up to a metre in length. The big leaf magnolia is quite rare in its native habitat in the south-eastern United States. In Britain it is seldom seen outside botanical institutions and arboretums. Its parchment-white fragrant flowers appear in early summer and can be over a yard across, but are often obscured by the leaves. Another large-leaved plant is *Rhododendron* 'Fortune', a cross between the two magnificent species *Rhododendron falconeri* and *Rhododendron sinogrande* made by Lionel de Rothschild at Exbury Gardens, in Hampshire. The huge yellow trusses of flowers appear in May. This grafted plant is now over twenty years of age, having been moved to Aberglasney as a semi-mature specimen in 1999.

Not all the planting is that exotic. I am very fond of the European spindle, *Euonymus europaeus*, which like the beech is more at home on shallow alkaline soils, but is very accommodating when planted outside its normal comfort zone. It really comes into its own during the autumn, when the foliage turns bright red and the scarlet seed-capsules reveal the bright orange-coated seeds.

The area is a peaceful place for visitors to wander and rest, with the sedating sound of the babbling stream always pleasantly audible. However, after heavy rain the water converges on the stream in torrents and becomes incredibly exhilarating. Birdlife is abundant in this area – we encourage it with nest-boxes – and visitors are guaranteed to see the redstart, the spotted flycatcher, and less frequently the pied flycatcher, gathering insects for their hatchlings during late spring and summer before they return to Africa.

There is still huge potential to develop this area yet further, but whatever is done must be very sympathetic so as not to spoil its existing magical atmosphere by over-zealous planting.

Opposite: An autumn view upstream before the clearance of the piggeries site in 2008.

Right: Part of Pigeon House Wood was planted with beeches in the nineteenth century.

THE SUNKEN GARDEN

'And now for something completely different,' as Monty Python would say. This is also something completely new. There never was a garden here. We have returned from Pigeon House Wood towards the mansion, but have sidestepped into an area surrounded on three sides by buildings from Aberglasney's old Home Farm – a range of one-storey bothies, a great slit-walled barn, and two estate workers' cottages, one of which originally housed the horse-drawn coaches. Both these have been converted into beautifully appointed holiday accommodation.

At first the staff used to park here. After an alternative parking area was created, it was time to turn this space into a garden. Time, as Lancelot Brown might have said 250 years ago, to consider the 'capabilities' of the site.

Left: Interesting and unusual evergreen plants with subtle charms, such as aromatic foliage, have been chosen for a low-key effect reminiscent of Japanese garden style in this new enclosed garden in a former farm courtyard. In principle the shrubs are compact and closely clipped, but here a spring flush of growth contributes additional colour.

Above: *Sarcococca confusa* is a useful, easy shrub. Its small flowers have a deceptively strong fragrance during the winter months.

Following pages: The shrubs in the Sunken Garden have been specially chosen for choice detail, occasionally enhanced by seasonal effects. The fruit of the South American or Andean blueberry *Vaccinium floribundum* in late summer (left), and (right) *Skimmia japonica* 'Red Riding Hood' during a harsh cold spell in January 2009.

Whatever the chosen scheme it had to be different from any other part of the garden, and ideally add yet another new dimension. The concept of a sunken garden was thought of long before the design was considered. The major problem was that half of the area remains in the shadow of a building for several months of the year, which limits the selection of plants that can be used.

For contrast in the formal 'courtyard' enclosure, curves were used to soften the rectangular frame. A garden like this would be unimaginable without some sort of water feature as focal point. Water is such a wonderful element in any garden design; it has so many properties – reflection, sound, movement – all of which create different moods. Something more than a simple pool seemed to be required here. William Pye is renowned for his imaginative water sculptures and was commissioned to design a feature for the Sunken Garden in 2004. An asymmetric

design using a square-and-circle theme was chosen, with a stainless steel hemisphere acting as the focal point, with running water rippling over the shining surface.

The trimmed evergreen planting that surrounds the central feature may seem a strange idea and some may consider it unexciting. The intention was to take inspiration from Japan. The combination of a calming green backdrop and flowing water is certainly not a new idea; many Japanese gardens have followed the same principle for hundreds of years. In the Western world, showy flowers have become the central emphasis in gardening. Japanese garden style puts the emphasis on form, foliage and structure, the result being a study in simplicity.

What this planting lacks in bright flower colour, it makes up in other, more subtle ways, by using evergreen plants that can be kept compact and have interesting characteristics. *Amomyrtus luma, Luma*

apiculata, *Luma chequen* and *Ugni molinae* all have aromatic foliage. *Sarcococca confusa, Sarcococca orientalis, Osmanthus delavayi, Osmanthus burkwoodii* and *Azara microphylla* all have inconspicuous flowers, but a wonderful fragrance. Of our five different blueberries, *Vaccinium floribundum*, the South American blueberry, is of particular interest as it is one of the few plants that is native to within a few miles of the equator, yet is hardy enough to flower in Britain. The explanation is that its home is high in the Andes, at elevations up to 4,000 metres.

It's almost as if visitors need to be educated in an appreciation of this planting. Visitors on a whistle-stop tour will often poke their noses into this area, quickly register the absence of conventional flower colour, and walk away to find something they consider more rewarding. I often want to take them by the arm and guide them back to open their eyes to the discreet charms of these carefully selected shrubby species. People who take the time to look carefully are also likely to be enraptured by the scents of both flowers and foliage – and by then, we hope, the calm, contemplative atmosphere of the garden will have begun to work its magic. I love to find people basking on the seats, with their thoughts away in a world of their own.

The plants are carefully trimmed two or three times a year to keep their undulating shapes. Their prostrate habit serves as a dense groundcover, so weeding is kept to a bare minimum.

Above: The North American blueberry *Vaccinium ovatum* with bright new red growth.

Opposite: *Gaultheria mucronata* 'Signaal', an ericaceous species native to Chile and Argentina.

CHAPTER SIX

THE NINFARIUM

This garden is not only a new creation, but also something entirely unique. It has even had a new name created for it – all of which calls for some explanation.

As you approach the mansion you can easily be deceived by the pristine face that it shows to the outside world, but the building could be said to have a split personality, and we have created a hidden garden in its hollow heart. The mansion once had an open central courtyard. The two principal façades which have been restored are the outward-looking ones; to the north is the formal approach to the house, and to the west, the wing that overlooks the Cloister Garden. The east and south wings are tucked into the hillside and were formerly the service wings. They fell into disrepair much faster than the more prestigious lived-in wings.

Much of this part of the building had lost its roof and its upper floors and lay open to the sky for nearly fifty years. This included the south-facing wing, which contained the early seventeenth-century kitchen, complete with fireplace, bread ovens and a cobbled floor, and an adjoining room to the west, which boasted a huge 1.5-metre wide fireplace.

With the exception of a very small area, the central courtyard had been encroached upon by Victorian improvements such as

Previous pages: The old kitchen transformed, soon after completion of the Ninfarium in the summer of 2005.

Right: *Phalaenopsis* orchids growing in an internal windowsill.

Left: Looking through to the south door of the Ninfarium, with *Passiflora racemosa* curtaining the wall.

bathrooms and storage rooms, which were more or less intact until very recently. We were left with a patchwork of stonework and windows, all of very different ages, but mostly structures of the nineteenth century. It was all very tumbledown, and there was no question of a complete restoration, as with the two principal wings.

The idea of glazing over and planting the ruinous inner courtyard of the mansion and the derelict south wing was conceived soon after I started work at Aberglasney for two reasons. Firstly, having worked with a collection of orchids and other tender plants in the past, I had a longing to have an area where I could grow them and display them to the public. Secondly, it would provide somewhere for visitors (and gardeners) to go to shelter from the rain and cold weather. However, because the area was so unstable I had my doubts that it would ever be possible. Matters were made worse when a large section of an interior wall collapsed in 1999, just at the time when we were all systems go to get the gardens ready for public opening. Thankfully this was a no-go area to both staff and builders and nobody was injured, but the collapse added considerably to the cost of the ongoing stabilization.

I have to confess that I never thought my dream would actually materialize because of the cost of bringing such a scheme to fruition. I remember discussing it at a subsequent meeting with Frank Cabot, who was decidedly enthusiastic about the idea. It turned out that from the start he too had nurtured a hope that the ruined servants' wing could be embellished with plants. His touchstone was the private garden in the ruins at Nymans in Sussex, but he also encouraged me to visit Ninfa, in Italy. Eventually through his magnanimous support and with assistance of some European funding, the idea became reality.

Ironically the major expense was not the covering of the ruinous courtyard and the construction of the garden within, but the exterior restoration of the very derelict east wing of the mansion. This was necessary to support the seriously heavy glass atrium roof.

The specification I required for the atrium roof was for it to be as transparent as possible, with clean simple lines, giving open views to the sky above. Work started in September 2004 by reducing the height of the crumbling walls, particularly the ones that ran east to west, to allow greater light penetration into what was to become the growing area. The east wing and the southeast tower were stabilized and roofed. The planning authorities considered our design the perfect solution, as it would have been absurd to rebuild the nineteenth-century additions, but the scheme retained the historical integrity of

Opposite: The dereliction of the roofless south and east service ranges was such that some walls had to be shored up with scaffolding, both inside and out. Once the fabric had been stabilized and the atrium roof built, the ground could be prepared for planting. Hollow blocks were laid to support the paved paths (top right) before the area was filled with compost.

Above: *Passiflora citrina*, a recent introduction from moist pinewoods in Honduras and Guatemala, is probably the only yellow passion flower pollinated by hummingbirds.

the building. The atrium roof was then skilfully built over the inner rooms.

Once the majority of the building was complete, the garden team moved in to start digging out the planting borders. We discovered that at a depth of 1.5 metres we were down to the natural water table, which can now be seen by looking down the well. This was quite exciting as it meant that the plants, particularly the large specimens, would be watered by capillary action from the moisture below. After all the beds had been dug out, they were backfilled with different types of compost, depending on what was to be grown in each particular area.

The battering at the base of the interior walls left very little room to backfill the planting beds with enough compost for the roots of the plants to grow well. To overcome this problem, the reclaimed Welsh blue Pennant sandstone slabs were laid on two

Left: Even at midwinter, evergreen foliage makes a magnificent architectural display.

Right: *Paphiopedilum* orchid hybrids growing in an old fireplace.

Following pages: Kahili ginger or *Hedychium gardnerianum* (left) needs winter protection in Britain, but in warmer climates like those of Hawaii, Jamaica and New Zealand, it has become one of the most problematic invasive alien species. *Gloriosa superba* (centre) is a climbing member of the lily family from tropical central and southern Africa. But danger lies in its dramatic beauty: all parts of the plant are highly poisonous. *Magnolia doltsopa* 'Silver Cloud' (right) is too tender to survive outdoors in this part of the country, but in an enclosed space like the Ninfarium, its beautiful felt-covered buds and strongly fragrant flowers can really be appreciated.

rows of hollow blocks and compost was placed underneath the path between the hollow blocks. This allowed the roots of the plants that grow against the wall to travel under the path into the larger planting beds in the centre of the rooms.

A thermostatically controlled electric heater is situated in the cellar. The warm air is piped underground and enters the Ninfarium through the old cast-iron drainpipes. During the summer months the same system is used to aid air circulation by blowing cool air through the pipes instead.

The project was completed ready for opening to much acclaim on 1 August 2005, but the new garden area needed a name. Several ideas came to mind, such as the Atrium Garden and the Courtyard Garden, both of which I suppose would have been

Left: Once peopled by scurrying servants and kitchen maids, the former service rooms and inner courtyard are now home to a wealth of exotic plants that luxuriate in the balmy conditions.

Right: The large flowers of birthwort, or giant Dutchman's pipe (*Aristolochia gigantea*), evoke comments from ornate and impressive to strange and sinister. Most of the 300 species of aristolochia have a putrid smell, but happily these flowers have a pleasant lemon scent.

Following pages: The long-lasting waxy flowers and intense fragrance of *Stephanotis floribunda* (left) have earned it the name Madagascar jasmine. It is not a true jasmine, however, since it belongs to the milkweed family Asclepiadaceae, rather than to the Oleaceae, as do species of *Jasminum*. *Passiflora racemosa*, the finest of all red passion flowers, also has attractive evergreen leaves (right). A native of Brazil, it has been in cultivation for many years.

adequate. However, the area was reminiscent of the stunning romantic garden of Ninfa, a town built at the foot of the Lepini Mountains 45 miles southeast of Rome.

The word 'Ninfa' came from a small Roman temple that once stood where the river Nympheus entered the garden and in Roman times was dedicated to nymph goddesses. Ninfa was once a prosperous town supporting seven churches and all contained within a double walled fortification. Its prosperity lasted for 600 years, from the eighth century until it was destroyed by the inhabitants of hostile neighbouring towns in 1381.

The garden at Ninfa covers an area of 21 acres, so the scale is very different from ours at Aberglasney, but anyone who has been to Ninfa or has seen photographs of the place would recognize the resemblance – a picture of crumbling stone walls swathed in luxuriant vegetation. Having chosen to pay tribute to Ninfa, we added '-arium', a suffix which usually denotes a place; examples are planetarium and vivarium. Thus we coined the name 'Ninfarium'. I do feel a little bit guilty when visitors tell me that they have spent ages trying to look up the meaning of the word to no avail. Who knows, one day it might be in a dictionary.

There is an old well in the Ninfarium, fed by a spring, in the corner of the old

Left: Bougainvillea and *Gloriosa superba* clambering over a ruinous wall in the Ninfarium.

Right: *Magnolia champaca* has a divinely powerful fragrance. It is used commercially to produce champak oil, a celebrated perfume of the East and an ingredient of the perfume 'Joy' created in 1930 by Jean Patou.

kitchen, but sadly I have not come across any nymph goddesses so far.

It is interesting to note that the garden at Ninfa, which was created by the Caetani family, has a connection with South Wales. Marguerite Caetani gave financial support to the Welsh poet Dylan Thomas, and her help and interest resulted in the first version of *Under Milk Wood*. Some people have mistakenly claimed that the wood in the play must be located near Aberglasney. The confusion arose because the play contains an oblique poetic allusion by the Reverend Eli Jenkins to 'Golden Grove 'neath Grongaer' – the hill to the west of Aberglasney that John Dyer made famous. At least the reference suggests that Dylan Thomas knew the neighbourhood hereabouts.

The excavation of the planting beds within the Ninfarium was one of the most difficult tasks of the operation. The mansion was wisely built on bedrock, but in places this necessitated the use of a pneumatic jackhammer to penetrate the rock to create the planting beds. The resulting stony spoil all had to be barrowed out of the narrow rear door and taken away a tonne at a time.

The choice of plants was determined by the temperature regime. Ideally I would have liked a tropical climate, but the cost of heating would have been prohibitive. The temperature is controlled so as not to go below 6 degrees Celsius. In the heat of the summer, vents open automatically in the roof and side windows to provide the necessary ventilation.

I had a clear idea in my mind of what I wanted to grow and in early 2005 it was thrilling making plant-hunting visits to nurseries to buy the plants. Many of the smaller specimens came from growers in the UK, but the large specimens were sourced from specialist nurseries in the Netherlands.

Among the prize trophies imported was

the Mexican *Dioon spinulosum*, which according to the *Guinness Book of Plant Facts and Feats* 'is claimed as the slowest growing flowering plant with a specimen found to be almost 1,000 years old and yet was only 2 metres in height. It is one of the most primitive of flowering plants and the only survivor of a once important part of the earth's vegetation.'

Another plant I am really fond of is the *Phoenix roebelenii* or pygmy date palm, which I bought at Naaldwijk near The Hague. I noticed a row of these palms at the nursery, all very uniform except one, which had a bent knobbly trunk, giving it more character, and looking almost reptilian. Hoping to get the price knocked down, I asked the nursery owner how much discount he would give me for the misshapen specimen. His answer was, 'because it is bent, it is more expensive'. You can but try! It is now growing happily near the well.

I really like the large-leaved foliage plants such as the *Strelitzia nicolai* and the bananas, which give the Ninfarium a tropical atmosphere. When the banana produced its first bunch of small, sweet bananas in 2006, they were given to the local artisan ice-cream maker in Llandeilo. I would imagine it was the first time banana ice-cream had been made commercially from bananas grown in the UK.

The high roof allowed room to plant large palms and trees of considerable height. Towering walls of every aspect made a perfect support to grow interesting climbers, and planting pockets were made in the crumbling old masonry walls to add further decorative touches with choice plants.

The banana passion fruit, as it is called, is a native of Columbia. Away from their natural hummingbird pollinators, the stunning flowers of *Passiflora antioquiensis* remain open for up to four days.

NOTE ON PHOTOGRAPHY

The Author's own photographs have been taken at Aberglasney using a Leica R8 35mm camera, using either Kodachrome 25 (now discontinued) or Fujichrome Velvia 50. Nearly all of the photographs were taken in the softer early morning or evening light. The slow film speed and long exposure times made it necessary to attempt taking pictures, particularly close-ups, only on the rare occasions when there was not a breath of wind.

I am very grateful to the following who have given me permission to use their photographs and images in this book:
Frank Cabot: pages 11, 17, 19 (above), 40, 62 (above) and 166 (above).
Kathy de Witt: page 34 (left).
Craig Hamilton: illustration page 28.
Rowan Isaac: page 43.
Frances Rankin: page 33.
Aberglasney Restoration Trust: page 186.

Fallen leaves of *Magnolia macrophylla*

INDEX

A

Aberglasney Restoration Trust 23, *30*, 31, 91, 163, 186

Acer (maple) 150

A. campbellii subsp. *flabellatum* var. *yunnanense* 150

A. griseum (paperbark maple) *154*

A. palmatum 'Red Filigree Lace' 150

A.p. 'Trompenburg' *143*

Achillea grandiflora 91

A. millefolium 50

Acidanthera murielae, see *Gladiolus murielae*

Actaea (previously *Cimicifuga*) 106

A. matsumurae 'White Pearl' *134*

Adiantum aleuticum 106

A. pedatum 106

Adoxa moschatellina (townhall clock) 100

Agapanthus africanus 73

A. 'Bressingham Blue' 73, *73*

A. campanulatus 'Oxford Blue' 73, *73*

alchemilla *69*

Aloysia triphylla (lemon verbena) 191

Alpinum 34, 158, 170–79

Amaranthus caudatus (love lies bleeding) *89*

Ammi majus (bishop's flower) 89

Amomyrtus luma 208

Anaphalis triplinervis 'Sommerschnee' 65

Anemone 35, 100

A. x *hybrida* 'Honorine Jobert' 65

A. nemorosa (wood anemone) *201*

apples 81, *82*

Arisaema 108, 126–9

A. candidissimum 128

A. consanguineum 128

A. fargesii 128

A. speciosum 127

Aristolochia gigantea 221

ash 190; weeping, see *Fraxinus excelsior* 'Pendula'

Asiatic Garden 142–57, 158

asters 89

Astilboides tabularis 130

Athyrium filix-femina 106

A. niponicum var. *pictum* 'Red Beauty' 106

Aviaries 95, 158, *160*, 162–9

Azalea 'Santa Maria' *143*

azaleas 145

Azara microphylla 208

B

bananas 227

Banksia 75

beech 196, *203*

Belgian Fence 76, *76*, 80, 91

Berllan Dywyll farm 158, 170

Bishop Rudd's Walk *34*,

Blechnum chilense 106

B. magellanicum 106

bluebells *196*, 201, *201*

blueberries, see *Vaccinium*

Bomarea 75

Borage (*Borago officinalis*) 82, *84*

Boston ivy *65*

Bougainvillea *224*

Bowles, E. A. 69, *75*

box (*Buxus*) *50*, 53, *53*, *57*, 72, 76, *82*, *187*, 191

Brown, Lancelot 'Capability' 17, 19, 205

brunnera 160

Byng family 50

C

Cabot, Anne 19, 20

Cabot, Frank 11, 19, 20, 76, 215

Cadw 47

Caetani family, 205; Marguerite 227

Camassia leichtlinii 'Semiplena' *57*, *69*

Camellia 154

C. 'Cinnamon Cindy' *145*

C. x *vernalis* 'Yuletide' *150*

C. rotundifolia 50

Capel Isaac 82

Cardiocrinum giganteum 99

Cerinthe major 'Purpurascens' (honeywort) 86

Chatto, Beth 100

Chelsea Physic Garden 75

Chimonanthus praecox var. *luteus* (wintersweet) *34*, *34*

Christie's 19, 31

Citrus aurantium (orange) 53

C. sinensis 53

Clarke, Gillian 33

Clerodendrum bungei 111, *134*

Cloister Garden 12, 19, 27, 28, 30, 32, 36–53, 58, 62, *182*, 212

cornflower 82

Cornus capitata 150

C. 'Eddie's White Wonder' 95

NOTE: NUMBERS IN *ITALIC TYPE* REFER TO ILLUSTRATIONS AND THEIR CAPTIONS.

Right: *Narcissus* 'Trena'

Left: *Maianthemum racemosum*

Opposite: *Rodgersia pinnata* (left) and *R.p.* Mount Stewart form (right)

PLAN OF ABERGLASNEY

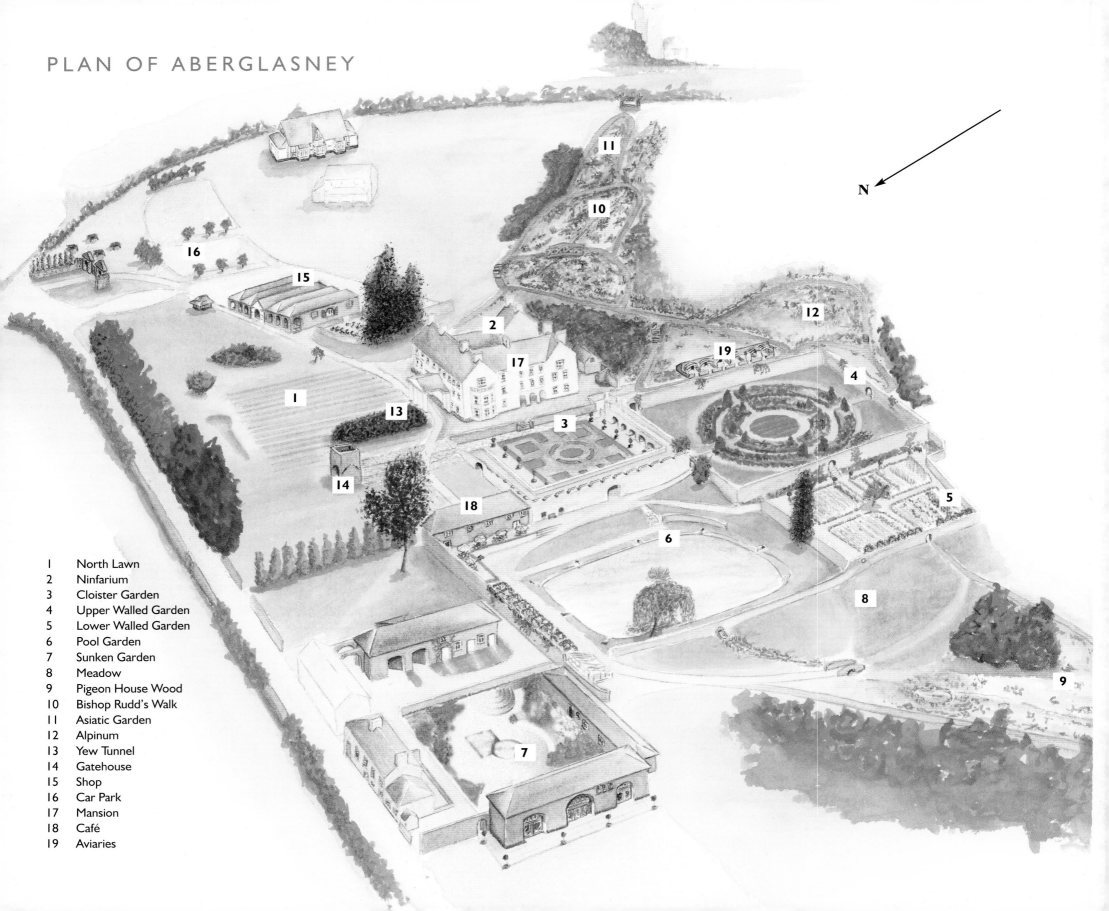

N

1   North Lawn
2   Ninfarium
3   Cloister Garden
4   Upper Walled Garden
5   Lower Walled Garden
6   Pool Garden
7   Sunken Garden
8   Meadow
9   Pigeon House Wood
10 Bishop Rudd's Walk
11 Asiatic Garden
12 Alpinum
13 Yew Tunnel
14 Gatehouse
15 Shop
16 Car Park
17 Mansion
18 Café
19 Aviaries